GOOD PROFIT

GOOD PROFIT

HOW CREATING VALUE FOR OTHERS

BUILT ONE OF THE WORLD'S MOST

SUCCESSFUL COMPANIES

CHARLES G. KOCH

CROWN
BUSINESS
NEW YORK

Crown Business books are available at special discounts for bulk purchases for sales promotions or corporate use. Special editions, including personalized covers, excerpts of existing books, or books with corporate logos, can be created in large quantities for special needs. For more information, contact Premium Sales at (212) 572-2232 or e-mail specialmarkets@penguinrandomhouse.com.

Library of Congress Cataloging-in-Publication Data is available upon request.

ISBN 978-1-101-90413-8
eBook ISBN 978-1-101-90414-5

Printed in the United States of America

Book design by Lauren Dong
Jacket design by Jess Morphew

10 9 8 7 6 5 4 3 2 1

First Edition

*I dedicate this book to Liz,
my wife of forty-three years. If I had searched the world
over I could not have found a better mate—
loving, supportive, smart, insightful, courageous, and
a constant source of joy.*

Contents

PART III

GOOD PROFIT

PART I

A Win-Win Philosophy

The possibility of men living together in peace and to their mutual advantage, without having to agree on common concrete aims, and bound only by abstract rules of conduct, was perhaps the greatest discovery mankind ever made.

—F. A. HAYEK[1]

P eace" and "mutual advantage": These are essential requirements for civil society and, on an individual level, for success—yours and mine. Together with those "abstract rules of conduct" so admired by Nobel Prize–winning economist Friedrich Hayek, they mirror the goal of my business management framework: that everyone knows the right thing to do and is motivated to do it—without explicit directions or overly detailed rules.

As CEO of Koch Industries, Inc., I am proud to work with principled people who help themselves by helping others improve their lives. I am dedicated to pursuing only a certain kind of profit—what we call "good profit."

By "good profit," I don't mean high margins or high return on capital, or lots of profit by just any means. What I consider to be good profit comes from Principled Entrepreneurship™—creating superior value for our customers while consuming fewer resources and always acting lawfully and with integrity. Good profit comes from making a contribution in society—not from corporate welfare or other ways of taking advantage of people.

The most value for customers is created by the scenario described by Hayek on the previous page. One that maximizes the freedom of the employees bound only "by abstract rules of conduct." This is how we strive to manage Koch Industries.

In the early 1990s when Koch Industries introduced its management framework, Market-Based Management®, to our metal fabrication plant near Bergamo, Italy, its union leaders responded with concern: "This might work in the United States, but it's not going to work in Italy. Here, managers think. Workers work. You're asking us to do the managers' job." Yet that mentality undermines success, general well-being, and the development and fulfillment of the individual.

We prefer to look at business through a win-win mind-set, which was the guiding philosophy behind the MBM framework we began to develop in the mid-1960s. This framework has enabled Koch to grow tremendously; indeed, it was essential to turning a company valued at $21 million in 1961 into one valued at $100 billion in 2014. (This $100 billion figure is derived from *Forbes*'s estimate of my brother David's net worth and my net worth.)

As shown on the next page, an investment of $1,000 in our company in 1960 would have a book value of $5 million today (assuming reinvestment of distributions)—a return 27 times higher than what a similar investment in the S&P 500 would have achieved.

It is worth noting that our rapid growth in value has continued even as we have grown into a large organization with more than 100,000 employees. Such results are uncommon among large companies. In 1917, for example, *Forbes* produced its first list of the hundred largest companies in the United States. Ninety-six years

KOCH'S GROWTH COMPARED TO THE S&P 500's

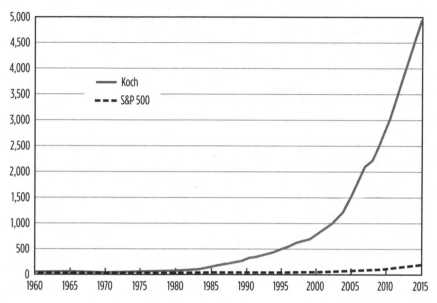

later, only thirteen of those companies were still in existence and independent, and only seven remained among the hundred largest in the country. Despite all their assets and capabilities, the vast majority of the nation's largest companies could not keep pace.

What is Koch's secret? I believe it is Market-Based Management, our unique business management framework, which has allowed us to more than keep pace through half a century of dramatic change.

In the decades since we began to develop this framework, energy prices have risen and fallen in repeated cycles, global competition has intensified, the geopolitical map of the world has been redrawn, the volume of regulation and litigation has soared, new technologies have transformed industries and businesses, and the pace of innovation has accelerated, but MBM has enabled us to deal with it all—all the while earning "good profits": good because they are driven by a voluntary, mutually beneficial relationship with customers. We don't lobby the government to mandate or subsidize what we're selling. That creates bad profit. Instead, we earn profit by creating value—for customers, society, our partners, and every employee who contributes. That is good profit.

Going forward, Koch's vision is to double profits on average every six years by applying Market-Based Management, which is outlined and detailed in this book's chapters.

Like most, I am interested in the well-being of not only my family and myself, but others as well. Clearly my family and I have benefited from the success of Koch Industries. But so have the more than 100,000 people Koch employs around the world in over sixty countries, including China, Mexico, India, Japan, Canada, the UK, Germany, Singapore, Brazil, and Malaysia—as well as all the people who have affordable access to countless valuable products and services because of Koch's efforts and discoveries.

This includes those who benefit from readily available, high-quality fuels (including biofuels) with which they power their businesses, heat and cool their homes, and fuel their vehicles. It includes those whose lives are now easier because of the innovations that make crops more productive, stretch denim jeans more comfortable, carpets more durable, and baby diapers more absorbent and elastic. It includes those who enjoy the health benefits of touchless hand towel and soap dispensers in public restrooms, and smartphones made smaller and lighter thanks to better connectors inside. We satisfy the customer's desire whenever we have the capability to do so, and the customer confirms that value by allowing us to profit. And there is much more value creation to come from Koch in the future.

In 2007, I explained our management framework in a book called *The Science of Success*. When I wrote it, the book value of Koch Industries (adjusted for distributions) was about two thousand times greater than in 1961 when I returned home to Wichita, Kansas, to work for my father. As I mentioned earlier, the adjusted book value is now five thousand times greater. Even during the Great Recession of 2008 and its aftermath (one of the worst economic periods since the Great Depression), Koch Industries more than doubled its shareholders' equity and increased its workforce by more than 40 percent.

Companies are always lobbying for special treatment, but during that recession a large number of them stepped up their pressure on the government for favors. They did so quite effectively—but at the expense of taxpayers and consumers, and to the rigged disadvantage of their competitors. Too often, Washington chooses winners and losers in the economy. This is corporate welfare, and it's the opposite of freedom and good profit. I have spent a lot of energy and resources speaking out about the dangers of profit by coercion, which is the antithesis of our Market-Based Management philosophy.

Market-Based Management emphasizes Principled Entrepreneurship over corporate welfare, virtue over talent, challenge over hierarchy, comparative advantage over job title, and rewards for long-term value creation over managing to budgets. MBM has enabled Koch to spread well-being to our employees, to all those who benefit from our products and services, *and* to all those who benefit from the resources conserved by our greater efficiency and creativity.

No one can decide which products and services a customer values better than the customer. Dedicating ourselves to satisfying what she values is showing respect for her. This is what generates good profit. Bad profit comes from disrespecting customers by making them subsidize our business with their tax dollars and higher prices, siphoning away the good profit other companies could have earned.

This is why our company opposes government subsidies, such as special tax breaks, import tariffs, restrictions on exports, mandates, anticompetitive regulations, and bailouts—including those that would seem on the surface to be beneficial to us. Corporate welfare relieves recipients of the constructive pressure to innovate and create value for society, hinders the unsubsidized competition by coercion, and limits the choices available to consumers.

Of course, when markets *are* distorted through corporate welfare, Koch is forced to deal with these distortions to remain competitive. For example, like virtually everyone, we take advantage of lawful tax breaks. Most subsidies, however—such as import tariffs, export restrictions, and anticompetitive regulations and mandates—are enshrined in law and are not optional.

We advocate the elimination of all these distortions, even those from which we currently benefit—such as ethanol mandates, restrictions on the export of crude oil and natural gas, and import tariffs. As an ethanol producer and large consumer of U.S. crude oil and natural gas, we profit *short term* from these market distortions. But rules like these—that don't lead to good profit—leave virtually everyone worse off *long term,* including us.

Free societies, which are based on respect for what people value, enjoy the greatest prosperity. Prosperous countries such as New Zealand and Switzerland, while not perfect, secure individual rights—including property rights—for all. They allow everyone to express ideas and markets to function freely—better than the great majority of the world's countries.[2]

Societies that don't embrace freedom wind up with the least prosperity. Venezuela is a country rich in natural resources, yet after just fourteen years under a socialist government, it now rations food, electricity, water, and other staples.

From antiquity to today, the best societies, as well as the best companies, have been the ones with a framework of freedom in which individuals can improve their lives by improving the lives of others.

This freedom enables entrepreneurs to discover how to best use resources to satisfy what people value through economic means. For example, when the technology to transmit data by optics rather than electricity was developed, transmission companies began switching from wire to fiber-optic cable, increasing capacity and speed, and freeing more copper to be used for other purposes. This greatly improved the cost, speed, and quality of transmitting images, voice, and data—thus generating good profit.

When economic signals are allowed to direct actions, people gain the knowledge of what is valuable to others and the magnitude of that value. They are then motivated to replace old systems with new ones that improve people's lives. This is why the world went from mainframe computers to laptops and tablets: not because of some government subsidy or mandate, but because consumers showed they valued the latter more than the former.

If the market signaled that consumers value energy from solar panels more than energy from oil and gas, the solar energy industry wouldn't need to pursue profit by political means as Solyndra did, in seeking subsidies from energy consumers and taxpayers. The solar power industry, like every business, should strive to profit by economic means instead of coercive ones.

At Koch, we stress the importance of incessantly embracing innovation and replacing old products, services, and methods with newer and better ones, such as Georgia-Pacific's touchless hand towel and soap dispensers. GP is now working on systems to prevent infections by alerting health-care workers if they neglect to sanitize their hands before treating a patient.

This is yet another example of our driving creative destruction (see chapter 3) and earning good profit from it, because reducing the spread of hospital infection may reduce the need for hospital beds and medicine. (Every improvement is bad for somebody's business, but no one can argue that fewer infections are a net negative for society as a whole.)

The superior petrochemical processes developed to make nylon by INVISTA are another example. INVISTA, acquired by Koch in 2004, is one of the world's larger producers of fibers, polymers, and chemical intermediates. We're working to replace some of its processes, and others, with more efficient biological ones, freeing up more resources to be used elsewhere. The new processes will result in reduced emissions, require less energy, and have fewer by-products.

These biological processes might bring disruption, rendering some of our existing plants obsolete, causing losses, and necessitating organizational change. But in the long run, old plants should be replaced by even better ones, and it is consumers and society as a whole that benefit from less expensive, more environmentally friendly nylon products in clothes, cars, and appliances. This generates profits for the entrepreneur who shares in the value created for the consumer.

MBM prompts us to focus on understanding consumers' unmet needs and finding ways to satisfy them. We strive to do this faster and better than existing and potential competitors. This requires that we continuously improve our existing capabilities, such as sales, marketing, operations, distribution, finance, technology, and R&D. MBM also requires that we add new capabilities faster than our competitors. For example, the acquisitions of INVISTA and GP allowed us to develop consumer marketing and branding capabilities that opened up new opportunities for existing businesses and future acquisitions.

When I'm asked to share our MBM principles with other businesses and organizations, I have done so willingly. I don't believe that others' success will diminish our own. On the contrary, MBM is win-win. But MBM is not a secret sauce recipe. It can't be relayed in a list of to-dos. Nor is it a package of think-outside-the-box slogans that can be implemented after a daylong seminar.

MBM is not just another buzzword management system that accomplishes nothing. "Eliminate slogans," demanded management theorist W. Edwards Deming after witnessing numerous factories filled with posters exhorting improvements of various kinds. To him, slogans just confirmed what employees already suspected: that management doesn't know what it's doing. We saw a great deal of merit in Deming's system, but found it was too limited to cover all the requirements for business success.

MBM helps employees better answer the question of "how" and then goes even further. It helps them address *what* the business should do to create the most value in society as well.

So the reader should be forewarned: MBM is extremely powerful, but successfully applying it is neither simple nor easy. After more than five decades spent developing and applying these principles at Koch, I've learned it is not enough to simply memorize the methodology or learn your way around the metaphorical toolbox. It's essential to understand the underlying principles sufficiently to be able to adapt those tools to fit the problem.

The successful application of MBM requires internalizing its principles at all levels of the organization, especially in leadership. If you've never swung a golf club or driven a car before, theory and instruction will only get you so far. You need to pick up a club or get behind the wheel and keep practicing until you internalize the mechanics to the point where you can do so automatically. It needs to become second nature to you. Similarly, MBM requires being able to conduct your business activities without even having to think about the mechanics of MBM.

Some key aspects of MBM, such as the emphasis on values and entrepreneurship, are legacies of my father, Fred Koch, a first-generation American. A self-made man and John Wayne–type figure, he exemplified much of what is at the core of our culture (and can't be imparted in a quick tutorial): the value of hard work, integrity, humility, and a lifelong dedication to learning. As his business became profitable, he spent his free time reading and ranching—not living a flashy lifestyle. Despite his intelligence, he was the kind of man who readily admitted what he didn't know, and prized honesty in all matters. He did his best to transmit those values to his sons.

Some previously published accounts of my teenage years describing me as rebellious and bullheaded are not entirely fictional. As an idealistic man in my twenties, I became passionate about the urgency of finding freedom-fueled solutions to human problems, even if the solutions were radical.

When I joined my father at work in 1961, I had two goals: One was helping to build a large, innovative, principled company focused on creating real value and earning good profit. My father's leadership had built the company up to a net worth of $21 million, and I thought we could improve on that. In fact, shortly after I joined, I plotted out my vision for the company's growth. (By 2013 we had exceeded my lifetime goal by seventyfold.)

My other goal was to discover the principles that best enable people to flourish as they live and work together. In this I was influenced by my mother, who had a deep sense of obligation to help everyone who reached out to her. She personified a principled regard for the community, which to me reflects Adam Smith's vision:

> And hence it is, that to feel much for others, and little for ourselves, that to restrain our selfish, and to indulge our benevolent affections, constitutes the perfection of human nature; and can alone produce among mankind that harmony of sentiments and passions in which consists their whole grace and propriety.[3]

For Smith, this ideal could only be achieved through voluntary restraint of one's selfishness. My father helped me see the adverse consequences of Communism's attempt to coerce this "perfection of human nature." I agreed with him about the horrors of Communism, which he witnessed firsthand while building plants in the Soviet Union under Stalin. But in the 1960s my philosophy about the role of government diverged from his.

This began to happen as a result of my spending most of Wichita's quiet nights reading and studying. Though an engineering major, I also studied mathematics, physics, and chemistry at MIT. I learned that we live in an ordered universe and that the natural world is governed by certain principles. To survive and prosper, people must understand and respect those principles. For example, Newton's third law is that every action has an equal and opposite reaction. (We ignore Newton's laws at our own peril.)

I began to wonder if there were, likewise, principles that determined societal well-being. I sought to read everything I could find on the subject from every relevant discipline, including history, economics, philosophy, science, psychology, sociology, and anthropology. What these disciplines had in common, I found, was that each explained how different social systems enhanced or diminished people's well-being. I studied the ancient Greeks and Romans, the medieval Scholastics, the Dutch Golden Age of freedom, the British Empire, and other major civilizations. As in the physical sciences, it became obvious that humans ignore at their own peril the fundamental principles of how to best live and work together.

My readings covered the entire philosophical spectrum from "left" to "right" and everything in between. I discovered my own political orientation was much more nuanced than simply "conservative" or "liberal," in the contemporary sense of those words.

Plato, Aristotle, John Locke, Adam Smith, Will Durant, Karl Marx, Vladimir Lenin, John Maynard Keynes, and Karl Popper all made tremendous impressions on me—some good and some bad. Authors such as F. A. Harper, Friedrich Hayek, Abraham Maslow, Ludwig von Mises, Michael Polanyi, and Thomas Sowell were particularly helpful to my understanding of the principles that govern well-being in society.

I vividly recall the first two life-changing books I came across: F. A. Harper's *Why Wages Rise* and Ludwig von Mises's *Human Action*.

"Baldy" Harper, once a professor at Cornell University, showed that coercing businesses to pay employees more than the value of their production doesn't lead to wealthier employees overall, as one might assume. Instead, it actually leads to unemployment, which then reduces production and everyone's well-being. Harper demonstrated that real wages are determined by the productivity of labor. Policies that undermine this relationship between productivity and wages can only undermine well-being. (For every action, there's an equal and opposite reaction.)

The greater the discrepancy between wages and production, the greater the resulting unemployment. This discrepancy can help turn a recession into a depression, as it certainly did in 1929 after President Herbert Hoover—among other mistakes—pressured employers to pay artificially high wages when prices were falling. Instead, human well-being is maximized by allowing voluntary arrangements between employers and employees—not coercive ones—to determine wages. The more productive an employee is, the more an employer will need to pay to retain him.

In another life-changing read of my youth, Mises (a New York University visiting professor) showed in unparalleled depth and scope that a free society based on scrupulous respect for private property, the consistent rule of law, and the right to freely exchange goods and services is the system most conducive to human well-being, progress, civility, and peace.

In his magnum opus *Human Action*, Mises constructs a brilliant vision of how people can best live and work together. He begins by building on the answers to basic questions such as "How do we know things?" and "How do we know what's true and what's right?"

The more books I read, the more passionately I embraced the truth that widespread human well-being demands a system that clearly defines and protects private property rights, allows people to speak freely without intimidation or legal repercussions, refrains from interference with private parties' agreements and exchanges, and allows human action—rather than arbitrary notions about how much things "should" cost—to guide prices.

Allowing people the freedom to pursue their own interests (within the limits of just conduct) is the best and only sustainable way to achieve societal progress. For individuals to develop and have a chance at happiness, they must be free to make their own choices and mistakes, rather than be forced to accept choices made for them by others.

As I digested this and went about my business, it dawned on me that these principles are fundamental to the well-being not only of societies—as I learned through my interdisciplinary studies—but also of organizations, which are essentially small societies. When encountering a challenge at work (such as a sunk cost or competitive disadvantage), I began responding with the principles of a free society in mind. And sure enough, one concept at a time, I saw that the principles that worked in society also worked in an organization.

The experience gained and lessons learned as we innovated, stumbled, succeeded, and grew have enabled our philosophy and practice of Market-Based Management to evolve and improve. We expect it always will.

Since *The Science of Success* was published, Koch has continued to adapt to creative destruction's challenges with passion and intensity. We have modified our vision, entered new businesses, built new capabilities, and greatly improved and expanded our innovation efforts. We have substantially increased the size of our workforce and more than doubled our stockholders' equity. All this has been made possible by a marked improvement in the understanding and application of MBM throughout our organizations.

We have made changes, not only to our vision, but to our entire approach to recruitment and management, our internships, university relationships, junior military officer outreach, trade school relationships, compensation system, opportunity origination networks, methods for achieving environmental and safety excellence, and MBM training and application programs. We've gained new value-enhancing capabilities through acquisitions such as Molex, a leading global provider of electronic connectors and systems, and through our many innovations. This book includes many important new concepts, insights, applications, and recommendations for introducing MBM that were absent from *The Science of Success*.

And unlike *The Science of Success*, this book includes guidance on how to apply MBM to your own organization, whatever it may be. It also provides direct answers to the questions (and misconceptions) about MBM and Koch—particularly our successes and failures.

What has remained constant since *The Science of Success* was published is our commitment to MBM. The goal is unchanged: to enable a business to create more value and drive creative destruction faster and better than any existing or potential competitors.

For that to happen, employees need to know what to do without being told—something my associates near Bergamo failed to understand at first. For MBM to be an effective framework for solving problems and capturing opportunities, a simplified structure is required. After much trial and error, we organized MBM into five dimensions: Vision, Virtue and Talents, Knowledge Processes, Decision Rights, and Incentives. Each of these will be explained in its own chapter, but here's a snapshot of all five:

- **Vision:** Our vision is based on what we believe is the role of business in society: providing products and services that customers value more than their alternatives while more efficiently using resources. Consequently, we strive to profit only from benefiting both our customers and society as a whole. (Again, this is what we call good profit.)
- **Virtue and Talents:** Having skills and intelligence is important, but we can hire all the brightest MBAs in the world, and if they don't have the right values, we will fail. Therefore, we hire based on values first—then talent.
- **Knowledge Processes:** One of our top priorities is impressing on new employees that not only is it permissible to challenge their bosses respectfully if they think they have a better answer, but that they have an obligation to do so. And supervisors have the obligation to create a culture that invites challenges.
- **Decision Rights:** Just like owners usually take better care of their property than renters do, when an employee "owns" well-defined areas at work, she takes greater pride and responsibility for outcomes. This greatly improves results—especially when the role is a good fit for her skills and abilities.

- **Incentives:** At Koch, anyone can earn more than his boss if he creates more value. Our goal is to motivate all employees to maximize their contribution, regardless of the role.

Another improvement in this book is the inclusion of case studies demonstrating these five dimensions. Through these examples it will become clear that MBM utilizes these concepts differently than most management literature does. For example, "vision" for Koch is not a static, one-time statement of goals and aspirations. It is a dynamic concept, always evolving based on continual examination of how we can use our capabilities in response to changing opportunities to create the most value for our customers and society.

When I joined my father's company in 1961, its vision was to limit its oil gathering activities primarily to Oklahoma. This mollified our principal customers, the major oil companies, and gave us the liquidity to pay the estate taxes upon my father's death. (This was a major concern of his since he believed he didn't have long to live.)

Then Sterling Varner, the number two person in the crude oil gathering business, worked with me to persuade my father to expand our vision beyond Oklahoma. The new vision required building new capabilities such as trucking, sales, and trading so we could pick up the discards of the major oil companies and identify niches in which we could outperform them. Later, as we spotted new opportunities to deliver value to our customers, we applied what we learned from crude oil gathering to gathering other commodities—first, natural gas liquids, and then natural gas itself.

This kind of virtuous cycle—which is central to our vision—hasn't stopped since. We are constantly improving our capabilities, building new ones, and finding new opportunities for which they can create value. This is a departure from the conventional wisdom of most companies, which stick to industries they know well.

To make our vision reality, we also apply the other four dimensions in a harmonious way. Just as the human body is more than a collection of organs, MBM is far greater than the sum of its five dimensions. When these five dimensions and their underlying concepts are understood holistically and applied in an integrated, mutually reinforcing manner, any business can be transformed. MBM increases an organization's vitality by helping all its members understand that they are here to create real value. MBM teaches them how they can do it and motivates them to do so.

I am writing this book for all business readers who are eager to move beyond anecdotes, buzzwords, and laundry lists and learn how to apply MBM to generate good profit for themselves, their companies, and for society at large. I want each and every reader's company to be as successful as Koch, because I believe we all benefit from the generative power of creative destruction. I hope this book will be even more effective than my first at helping all readers further their understanding and application of MBM to maximize their contributions, realize their full potential, and benefit themselves by benefiting others.

Another very important audience for this book is Koch employees—present and future—who want to know how they can succeed. At Koch we have found that each employee can help us experiment and improve our ability to get results through MBM. In fact, employee innovations and contributions constitute most of the examples in this book.

Anyone concerned with improving human well-being can find value in this book by learning that much of what is done coercively—in the name of making people better off—does the opposite. Adam Smith put it best: "By pursuing his own interest [an individual] frequently promotes that of the society more effectually than when he really intends to promote it."[4]

Koch Industries' success has attracted growing interest in what we do and how and why we do it—both from admirers and critics. This scrutiny has been compounded by the increased visibility of our efforts to educate and mobilize people to advocate for market-based policies that improve human well-being for everyone in society, especially the most disadvantaged.

You may ask, as many have, "Why should Charles Koch care about helping others succeed?" Of course, the development and flourishing of Koch employees is in my own self-interest. But for me, helping the disadvantaged (who are the most vulnerable to ill-advised government practices and policies) lift themselves up is just as important. Why do I want another individual or business or organization to improve? The answer is because all of us benefit when others profit in a principled way.

MBM is valuable because it has a proven track record of success at Koch, and is based on consistent, valid theory that is fully integrated and applied across every aspect of the organization. It certainly has worked well for Koch Industries, and there's no reason it cannot work well for other organizations, too. I believe this book will benefit any principled individual or organization striving to create real long-term value, no matter their industry, profession, or trade.

I am convinced the proper implementation of our market-based philosophy has been the primary source of our success. But past performance does not guarantee future results. To continue to achieve superior performance and good profit, we must continually improve our understanding and application of MBM.

Just as a market economy continually experiments with better and better ways to provide people with what they value yet never reaches stasis, so MBM is a never-ending process of learning and improvement. To all readers of this book who endeavor to understand and apply these principles—for the good of their businesses and the well-being of mankind—I wish you every success on the journey.

CHARLES G. KOCH
Wichita, Kansas
July 2015

CHAPTER 1

The Glorious Feeling of Accomplishment

LIFE LESSONS FROM MY FATHER

I should regret very much to have you miss the glorious feeling of accomplishment and I know you are not going to let me down. Remember that often adversity is a blessing in disguise and is certainly the greatest character builder.

—FRED KOCH[1]

You can tell the Dutch," my father would joke about himself, "but you can't tell them much." Square-jawed, determined, and persistent certainly described Fred Koch, who plunged headfirst into countless ventures—some profitable, some not. His own father, Harry, was also a risk-taker—emigrating as a teenager from the Netherlands with very little money and a head full of stories about America's "Wild West."

Whether their reputation for stubbornness is deserved or not, the Dutch emerged from Spanish rule in 1581 with a thirst for peace, tolerance, knowledge, and new ideas. During the Dutch Golden Age of the seventeenth century, they created the first stock exchange, generated the highest standard of living in the world, excelled in arts and science, and sustained a flourishing culture. The

Dutch thrived thanks to freedom and a system of mutual advantage, while their less free European neighbors endured bloodshed and poverty.

Harry Koch arrived in New York as a printer's apprentice and brushed up on his English skills while working at Dutch newspapers in Michigan and Chicago. His work led him to travel down the Mississippi to Louisiana, and then to Trinity, Austin, and Galveston, Texas. In 1891 he followed the railroad to Quanah, where he bought a print shop and struggling weekly newspaper called the *Chief*. Quanah was in a very poor area, so many of Harry's customers paid, in part, with barter. They valued the news and advertising space his paper offered, and he valued their patronage. In an example of good profit at work, what is now the *Tribune-Chief* is still published today.

Harry had a thick Dutch accent and pronounced the name "Koch" with a soft, guttural "ch." The West Texan pronunciation sounded more like a crow's "caw." Years later, someone paged my father at a train station and mispronounced his name over the microphone as "Fred Coke." My father had never liked the West Texas version, so he adopted that pronunciation on the spot, thereby making a significant contribution to American phonology.

Fred played varsity football for Quanah's high school, and was an excellent orator and student. He attended the Rice Institute in Houston (an all-scholarship school at that time), where he was elected class president. Always ready to take any risk that might pay off, he transferred to MIT in Cambridge, Massachusetts, upon learning it had created the first-ever chemical engineering program. MIT's tuition at the time was about $300 a year. Before he moved from Texas to Boston, Fred spent the summer mopping decks on a tramp steamer—a merchant ship with no set schedule—sailing between New York and London.

Chemical engineering suited Fred Koch. His bachelor's thesis at MIT addressed environmental issues at a paper mill in Bangor, Maine, which was, coincidentally, later owned by Georgia-Pacific. (GP sold that mill but still owns the Acme gypsum plant near Quanah where my father held a summer job.) The opportunities presented by the Bangor mill—including the profitable recycling of waste products as well as energy conservation, both of which improved the environment—were important to my father and remain important to Koch, because they are mutually beneficial to our company and our communities.

At MIT, Fred, having been taught by his father to box, became captain of the boxing team. While my mother—a golfer, fly fisher, hunter, and jewelry designer—possessed excellent eye-hand coordination, Fred more than got by on his quick reflexes and competitive spirit. He encouraged all four of his sons to develop some boxing skills.

While boxing is one of my favorite Olympic sports, none of us pursued it. My brother Frederick always preferred the arts to athletics, eventually studying humanities at Harvard and drama at Yale. I had some of the most fun of my life playing rugby at MIT on a team that won two championships. My brothers David and Bill joined the MIT basketball team. David became its captain and was a small college all-American. In 1962 he set a record by scoring 41 points in one game—a record he held for forty-six years.

After college, my father got a job with Texaco (then called the Texas Company) as a research chemist at its refinery in Port Arthur, Texas. He then worked briefly as a chemical engineer for the Gasoline Products Company, a leading refinery process development firm in Kansas City.

Fred's big break as an engineer came in 1924, when his MIT classmate, Carl de Ganahl, recommended him for a job designing and constructing a refinery in England owned by de Ganahl's father, Charles. Like the Kochs, the de Ganahls had emigrated from Europe in the 1800s and eventually settled in Texas.

Charles de Ganahl was an amazing person—an outstanding entrepreneur with great integrity and compassion. His mentorship of my father, who was a twenty-four-year-old with very little business experience and even fewer connections, changed Fred's life. My father had tremendous respect for de Ganahl, so much so that he named me after him. That respect was mutual. "Fred Koch is the soundest chemical engineer in the world," de Ganahl wrote years later, "with as brilliant a pair of brain lobes as are worn by any young man of my acquaintance."[2]

My father gravitated toward quality people and genuinely made a good impression on them—whether it was the wealthy de Ganahl family or Sterling Varner, whose father and grandfather were oilfield mule contractors. He didn't care about social status; he treated everyone in a manner consistent with his values. It's probably a reflection of his character that good people wanted to be around him too and offered him opportunities for work.

In 1925, Fred's MIT experience, brilliant lobes, and way with people paid off again. Another former classmate, Dobie Keith, invited him to join an engineering and construction firm in Wichita, Kansas, which Keith had started with Lewis Winkler. Fred accepted, paying $300 to become an equal partner. Three months later, after Keith abruptly left to pursue another opportunity, the Winkler-Koch Engineering Company was formed.

The first two years were rough for Winkler-Koch. Because the firm lacked any proprietary technology or the capital to sell complete jobs (entailing design, equipment purchase, and construction management), small engineering fees were all Winkler-Koch could command. For a while my father was, as he put it, "dead broke" and had to sleep on a cot in the office.

Business improved in 1927 when Fred developed a better thermal cracking process for converting heavy oil into gasoline, one that was less expensive, provided higher yields, and involved less downtime than competitive processes. After a successful installation at L. B. Simmons's new Rock Island refinery in Duncan, Oklahoma, Winkler-Koch sold an average of one new installation every seven weeks for the next two years.

Winkler-Koch's success in selling this process to independent refiners inevitably caught the attention of the major oil companies, who had pooled their gasoline-making processes to control the technology. This combine, dubbed the Patent Club, charged the independents a royalty of 30 cents per barrel at a time when gasoline sold for a little over $3 per barrel (retail).

My father's new process, by contrast, was royalty-free, further enhancing its appeal to independent refiners. In 1929, the Patent Club—worried about the increased competitiveness of independents—filed forty patent infringement suits against Winkler-Koch and almost all its customers. These suits crippled the company's business in the United States and in much of Europe.

Winkler-Koch's survival as a company depended on building plants in other countries—particularly the Soviet Union, where it constructed fifteen cracking units between 1929 and 1931. As a result of that Soviet contract, Winkler-Koch enjoyed its greatest financial success during the early years of the Great Depression. Even so, Fred was very suspicious of the Soviets and demanded 90 percent payment up front.

The Soviet engineers who worked with my father confirmed his fears about doing business in the Soviet Union (and of Communism in general) when they told him about their methods and plans for world revolution. Stalin eventually purged almost all of Fred's Soviet counterparts, along with tens of millions more of his own people. My father described the Soviet Union as "a land of hunger, misery and terror." Because of his experiences there, he became a staunch anticommunist for the rest of his life—even joining the John Birch Society and encouraging me to as well. (I agreed but only stayed for a few years because I felt, like Hayek, that Communism was more of an "intellectual error" than a conspiracy that needed to be exposed.)

The Patent Club spent twenty-three years suing Winkler-Koch but was successful only once. And even that verdict was overturned after it was discovered that a judge had been bribed. This shocking behavior and the resulting scandal caused the majors to donate their process development company, Universal Oil Products, to the American Chemical Society. Winkler-Koch countersued, settling in 1952 for $1.5 million.

Despite winning, my father's advice to me was: "Never sue—

the lawyers get a third, the government gets a third and you get your business destroyed." I've tried to follow his advice and have filed very few lawsuits. Unfortunately, he forgot to tell me how to keep from *being* sued—even by members of my own family. But more on that later.

THE FOUNDING OF KOCH INDUSTRIES

The late 1930s brought more hard times for my father's engineering business. The Great Depression was ongoing, and the Patent Club lawsuits prevented him from reaping benefits from his thermal cracking process in the United States. So Fred stepped up his search for other business opportunities.

Once again, his good reputation served him well. Globe Oil and Refining Co. (one of the largest independent refiners and one of Winkler-Koch's best customers) decided to build a 10,000-barrel-per-day refinery on the Mississippi River near Wood River, Illinois, about fifteen miles upstream from Saint Louis.

Globe's owner, I. A. O'Shaughnessy, wanted partners to reduce the risk and bring additional capability to the venture. He first attracted Hank Ingram, owner of one of the largest barge fleets on the Mississippi, who could facilitate movement of crude oil and products in and out of the refinery. He then approached Fred to design and operate the plant.

My father agreed, on the condition of owning a substantial interest in the company. Fred paid $230,000 in 1940 for 23 percent of the Wood River Oil and Refining Co., Inc., the company that would eventually become today's Koch Industries. O'Shaughnessy and Ingram each owned 33 percent, and two Globe employees (involved in crude oil supply and product sales for Wood River) owned 5 percent each. The refinery was completed and began operating in 1941. Its owners could not have known what would come next.

World War II prompted Congress to pass four "excess profit" tax bills between 1940 and 1943, with rates ranging from 25 percent to 95 percent. As a result, during the war years, Wood River's income tax rate averaged nearly 70 percent.

This confiscatory rate did not prevent the government from pressuring Wood River to produce ever-larger quantities of high-octane aviation fuel. Also, like every other resource at the time, crude oil was difficult to obtain because of wartime shortages. No surprise, then, that conflicts arose among the primary stockholders.

One of those conflicts was inherent in the structure of the deal: The employees of Globe Oil who supplied crude oil for its refineries and those who sold Globe's products were to also help supply and assist sales for Wood River. This caused suspicion among the non-Globe partners that Wood River wasn't receiving equal treatment. Whether this was true or not, the lesson is that whenever conflicts of interest are built into an agreement, it is unlikely to work—for long. In 1944 the Globe Oil group agreed to transfer their shares at cost to my father and Ingram to settle the differences. Fred and Ingram became equal owners as a result.

In 1946, Wood River acquired the 8,000-barrel-per-day Rock Island refinery in Duncan, Oklahoma, and its 10,000-barrel-per-day crude oil gathering system (gathering systems transport crude oil from the wellhead to a major pipeline) for $600,000, plus the right for L. B. Simmons, Rock Island's owner, to purchase a 10 percent interest in Wood River. These assets were placed in a new subsidiary named Rock Island Oil and Refining. Although the Oklahoma refinery was shut down in 1949, its gathering system became the foundation for Wood River's largest business.

Wood River lost money in 1949, prompting the sale of its Illinois refinery to Sinclair Oil for a gain of $4 million. That sale enabled a buyout of the remaining stockholders, except for my father and L. B. Simmons (who had exercised his option to buy stock). They kept the Wood River name and in early 1954 made plans to build a new refinery near Chicago, but soon gave up on the idea.

My father was smart, entrepreneurial, successful, respected, and principled. And yet he was unfailingly humble. In 1948, he wrote to a friend in Pittsburgh, "This oil business of ours has grown so big that it needs a smarter man and a better organizer to handle it."[3]

Fred suffered physically, not just from the high blood pressure and heart problems that would eventually take his life. In 1940, a doctor suspected a growth on my father's palate was malignant and treated it with radium needles that destroyed the roof of his mouth. After that, Fred's speech deteriorated, and eating in front of others became painfully embarrassing for him. He worried he would need a new business—one that wouldn't require much interaction with others. Ranching seemed to fit that bill.

So in 1941 he bought most of the acreage for what became Spring Creek Ranch in the Flint Hills of Kansas, where he planned to work in isolation. "It was just a dreadful experience," my mother recalled four decades later.

"He couldn't work. He couldn't do anything." My mother was a very sensitive person who took others' suffering to heart. "He lived that way and didn't complain, but he would tell me sometimes, when he couldn't stand the pain," she said.

Thankfully a gifted doctor in Saint Louis found a way to repair my father's palate, and he slowly recovered. Spring Creek then served a much happier purpose for Fred. He became fascinated by the science of ranching and would spend weekends there with all of us staying in the family cabin. Among other innovations, he helped develop the artificial salt lick, an inexpensive way to ensure cattle got sufficient salt.

My father took on new interests easily and often, but not systematically: fiberglass pipe, camping trailers ("Koch Kampers"), and cooling towers for homes were a few of his diverse ventures in those years. After marveling at the uses of asbestos on a trip to South Africa, he considered getting into that business. (Thank goodness he didn't.) He even retrofitted a small fleet of World War II bombers into corporate aircraft.

Fred also worked on developing distillation tower internals

(trays used in refineries and chemical plants to separate liquids by boiling-point differences), inventing an especially ambitious one called the Kaskade Tray—which, unfortunately, turned out to work better upside down than right-side up. My father could laugh at himself, and he had to about that one.

None of these new ventures was ever successful. But the fact that he started with nothing in 1925 and built a company worth $21 million when I joined it in 1961—using nothing but that brilliant "pair of brain lobes"—is impressive. As his prosperity grew, he bought his parents a nice house in Quanah and supported them for the rest of their lives. Together with my mother, he managed to raise four rambunctious boys: Frederick, born in 1933, me in 1935, and fraternal twins David and William in 1940.

In a 1948 letter written to a friend in Pittsburgh, my father described Frederick as "quite a brilliant youngster . . . He has a fine mind and is very outstanding in his artistic gifts." Indeed, Frederick became an art collector and has restored several historic mansions around the world.

Papa, as we called him, described me as a "big, good natured kid," but my work ethic didn't yet impress him. "Everybody likes Charles and nothing worries him as long as work doesn't come too close."[4]

"Of the twins," my father wrote, "David is very quick in mind and body. He is a natural athlete and very practical. If any of the kids becomes an engineer, I think it will be he."

The other twin was William (called Bill), whom my father described once as having "a very lovable disposition but very high temper, coupled with terrific stubbornness. I suppose it is the result of his mixture of Irish and Dutch ancestry."

"Children in a family are far more important than making money," my father wrote to a friend in Texas the same year. He closed that letter with his characteristic humor, poking fun at John D. Rockefeller: "Mr. Rockefeller says 'Money isn't everything. There are stocks and bonds and other securities.' "[5]

FAMILY LIFE

Of course Papa was not the only parental influence on us boys. But while my mother might have been nicknamed "Mighty Mary" because of her boundless energy and adventurous streak, my father was the dominant force in our household. His character was unquestionable.

I remember a trip to the movies with him and my brothers in the 1940s. When we arrived, those already gathered at the box office had failed to form a straight line. My brothers and I began trying to improve our position so we'd be sure to get tickets. But my father, who was always teaching integrity, wouldn't have it. He signaled to us to regroup at a position near the back of the crowd.

Our father vowed he wouldn't allow his sons to become "country club bums," so he did whatever he could to ensure we developed a work ethic and thirst for knowledge. When I opened his safety deposit box shortly after his death, I discovered a letter he had written in 1936 expressing his concern that the insurance policies left us to pay for our education might be a detriment rather than a benefit:

> You can use it as a valuable tool for accomplishment or you can squander it foolishly. If you choose to let this money destroy your initiative and independence then it will be a curse to you and my action in giving it to you will have been a mistake. I should regret very much to have you miss the glorious feeling of accomplishment and I know you are not going to let me down. Remember that often adversity is a blessing in disguise and is certainly the greatest character builder.[6]

Frederick didn't react well to physical labor as a method of developing a work ethic, so I bore the full brunt of my father's efforts. By the time I was six, he made sure work occupied most of my spare time. I started out digging dandelions on our 160-acre property, then graduated to shoveling out horse and cow stalls, baling hay, and milking cows. These activities were followed by a job moving steel sheets around in the Koch Engineering shop.

By age fifteen, I was deemed old enough to enjoy a whole assortment of summer jobs at our ranches and elsewhere, such as rounding up and treating sick bulls, fixing fences, digging ditches and post holes in ground that hadn't seen a drop of rain in years, shoveling wheat in a grain elevator, and the like.

One summer I worked at a line camp in Montana's Centennial Valley, miles from anything. I bunked with a gentleman called Bitterroot Bob, who bragged about being dishonorably discharged from the military during World War II for running from the line of fire. Some nights he would fire his revolver through the roof of our log cabin. When it rained we'd both get wet, but that didn't seem to deter him. There was to be no country club for me in my youth.

Although it didn't seem so at the time, I'm now convinced my pop's tough love saved me. The truth is, I wasn't that easy to deal with. Being a free spirit, I had already attended eight schools by the time I graduated from high school. Years later, I asked my father why he hadn't been as tough on the twins as he was on me. "Son," he said, "you plumb wore me out."

One of the many schools I attended was a Catholic school, to which I was sent at age five for a couple of years. But I was a skeptic even at that young age. I rejected the nuns' claim—which I took literally—that Jesus was behind the altar. They offered graham crackers and milk as a reward for good behavior, but the incentive wasn't strong enough for me.

Fast-forward to my eighth school, Culver Military Academy, from which I was expelled in my junior year for drinking beer on the train from Wichita to Indiana during my return from spring break. Because I was contrite, Culver agreed to readmit me, on the condition that I make up the entire semester's academic work, plus all the standard cavalry drills, during summer school.

That summer I lived in a tent next to the horse barn. My work-load was four times that of the other summer cadets, so I would get up in the middle of the night to use the only light source permitted after taps: the one in the barn's communal bathroom, where I would sit on a shower bench and complete my homework.

My senior year, I crossed the line again by attempting to bang the head of the cadet captain—who was also the star running back of the football team—against my window. (He had pulled all my clothes out of my closet and thrown them on the floor during a room inspection.)

Fortunately, they didn't expel me a second time, as I had earned honors privileges by then. Also, graduation was right around the corner, and I had already been accepted at MIT. But I did lose my honors privileges and had to spend all my free time for the final six weeks of school walking post with my rifle.

During my brief expulsion from Culver, my father sent me to live with his brother's family in Texas to complete the academic year at Quanah High School. Math had always come naturally to me, and I remember correctly answering all ten questions on the math final. My classmates in Quanah were incredulous. Why would I exert myself when 70 percent answered correctly would have been passing? Despite being an independent-minded and occasionally rowdy teenager, I recognized something was not right with that mentality.

I entered MIT with no intention of returning to Wichita to work for my father. My independent streak wouldn't be a good match for his domineering style. (I knew by then that his "can't tell the Dutch much" joke was really no joke.) Nor was I the heir apparent to his company. He never gave any indication that he wanted my involvement other than requiring me to work in all my spare time.

At the end of my sophomore year, my grade average hovered around a B minus, which I thought was okay. (I was having a very good time in Boston, finally liberated from the regimentation of military school. MIT only required students to pass tests and complete projects, so I took full advantage of my new freedom.) But when I briefly returned to Wichita at the summer break, my father sat me down and said, "Son, I don't give a damn if you end up digging ditches for a living, but if you want me to pay for your education, you're going to apply yourself." Miraculously, my grades jumped a full point.

During my final semester at MIT, my father acquired a 35 percent interest in the Great Northern Oil Company, which owned the Pine Bend refinery near Saint Paul, Minnesota. Pine Bend had been built in the mid-1950s to provide a market for the sour, heavy Canadian crude oil recently discovered in Saskatchewan. Given the benefit of hindsight, it would be difficult to overstate the importance of this transaction to the future of Koch.

The driving force behind Great Northern was two independent oil companies—both of which were large producers in the Saskatchewan field—and J. Howard Marshall II, a prominent oil industry attorney and leader. By the late 1950s, the two independents had been acquired by Pure Oil and Sinclair Oil. Ike Moore, the former head of sales for Wood River, had worked for Sinclair ever since it bought the Wood River refinery in 1950.

Moore knew that Fred had a desire to get back into the refining business, so when Sinclair Oil decided to sell its share in Great Northern, Ike let Fred know of the opportunity. My father ended up buying Sinclair's interest, sight unseen, at book value: $5 million. His instincts and judgment proved right. At the time (February 1959), Pine Bend was running about 35,000 barrels per day, a little more than one-tenth of its capacity today.

That summer, Wood River Oil and Refining Co., Inc., changed its name to Rock Island Oil and Refining Co., Inc. Rock Island's businesses amounted to little more than ranching, the crude oil gathering system acquired from L. B. Simmons, and the newly purchased interest in Great Northern. Back then, Koch Engineering was a separate entity with a single plant in Wichita making just one product—a new tower internal innovation called the Flexitray®—which, unlike the Kascade Tray, became very successful.

AN OFFER I COULDN'T REFUSE

After finishing at MIT in 1959, I stayed in the Boston area for a few years working in product development, process development, and management services for Arthur D. Little, a leading consulting firm at the time. The nature of my work qualified me for an occupational deferment from the draft. (One interesting project was designing a plant for the government to produce a potent marijuana derivative. The idea was to make war more humane by controlling opponents with marijuana "bombs" rather than with weapons.)

Marijuana bombs notwithstanding, this was work I found stimulating and educational. Even though I was only in my midtwenties, I was frequently presenting to CEOs of firms. I was enjoying life and was very content to remain in Boston. But then my father made me an offer I couldn't refuse. After nearly a year of failing to coax me to return to Wichita to work under him, he delivered an ultimatum: His health was poor, and if I didn't come back to learn to run the company, he would have no choice but to sell it.

I'm not sure what prompted that ultimatum, though I now believe he had been counting on me to succeed him for some time. Perhaps it was my successful work at Arthur D. Little that had convinced him I had a strong business aptitude. He was certainly aware of my work ethic, thanks to the years of manual labor he had put me through. My older brother, Frederick, had never shown any interest or aptitude in engineering or business. And while my twin brothers were studying engineering at MIT, they were five years behind me and not yet done with their studies. So perhaps my father's offer was inevitable.

What I know for sure now is that our father feared he wouldn't be around much longer to run the company. He promised he would allow me to run Koch Engineering—the struggling tower internals business—without interference. Anything short of selling it would not require his permission. This was my chance to actually run a company instead of just advising one, so I accepted.

When I returned to Wichita in the fall of 1961 with an undergraduate and two master's degrees in engineering (nuclear and chemical) and over two years of consulting experience, my father's first words to me were "I hope your first deal is a loser; otherwise you will think you're a lot smarter than you are." He had nothing to worry about—I would get us into plenty of losers over the years. (More on those later.)

At that time, Koch Engineering had less than $2 million in sales and was barely breaking even. Its business in Europe was a mess. My father had planned to clean it up himself, but since I would be running Koch Engineering, he told me I should fix it. Too ignorant to know all the issues involved in building a successful business, especially an international one, I was eager to go over and tackle the problem.

Luckily, the problems with our European business were so obvious that even I could cure them, despite never having run a business or worked overseas.

The mess had been caused by our efforts to prevent potential competitors from copying our designs for tower internals. Multiple contractors were manufacturing different components in various countries, which were then assembled elsewhere, resulting in unwarranted complexity, high cost, and poor performance.

Over the next several years, I spent a great deal of time in Europe implementing my solution, which was twofold. First, we set up our own engineering and manufacturing site near Bergamo, Italy (home of the doubting union members).

Second, we built an organization that would provide superior service to our customers. From my work at Arthur D. Little and all my studies, I had a clear understanding that the purpose of business was to create value for customers. I had read enough business literature to know that if you couldn't satisfy your customers, you had no business. As Sam Walton famously said, "There is only one boss—the customer. And he can fire everybody in the company from the chairman on down, simply by spending his money somewhere else."[7]

THE SHOULDERS OF GIANTS

To his credit, my father was true to his word and gave me almost complete freedom in running Koch Engineering. After reorganizing our European business, I was sent to Saint Paul in 1962 to work at the Great Northern Oil Company for six months and to learn the refining business. After returning to Wichita, I continued to make frequent trips to Europe to push that transformation further.

While I was at Koch Engineering I learned the importance of vision (because we really didn't have one) and the importance of having the right people in the right roles (because we didn't). At twenty-seven, I replaced the president, which needed to be done and was in keeping with my father's promise to let me run the company using my own judgment.

I immediately began working to build the non-European parts of Koch's business, improving sales and manufacturing, and adding other products. One of my first steps was to bring in a commercial development person to help us add new products. Obviously, as president I was in an even better position to build Koch Engineering.

And build it we did; by 1965 its sales had more than doubled, taking the company from breakeven to solid profitability. From the outset I used an approach that is central to MBM—understanding and constantly improving and adding to our capabilities, and pursuing the opportunities for which they can add the most value.

In addition to setting up our own manufacturing in Europe and a new plant in Wichita (which led to improved marketing, sales, design, and manufacturing of Flexitrays worldwide) we got into related product lines, such as tower packing, heat exchangers, mist eliminators, pollution control equipment, and membrane separation systems.

Nineteen sixty-two was also the year I began working to expand Rock Island's largest business, crude oil gathering. My ally in this effort was Sterling Varner, whom I first met as a teenager during my summer in the Centennial Valley. Sterling shared my expansive vision for Koch. We aggressively bought crude oil trucks, trucking companies, and pipelines, and we built pipelines where others refused to take risks. "Watch out!" said a major oil company official. "If you turn your back, Koch will build a pipeline up your a**." We took that as a compliment.

As the growth of our crude oil gathering business accelerated, my father's fragile health deteriorated. In 1966 he made me president of Rock Island so that, as he put it, there would be no question about succession should anything happen to him. In May of the following year he had a severe heart attack that put him in the hospital for two months. A second, that November, was fatal.

On July 1, 1968, we renamed Rock Island in his honor and our company has been known as Koch Industries ever since. I still feel blessed to have worked with my father for those six years. Often when we see farther it's not because of our own keen sight but, as Isaac Newton said, because we stand on the shoulders of giants. In his own unique way, Fred Koch was such a giant.

Virtually all of us learn lessons from our parents, and I'm no different. My lessons weren't specific to business, but they were fundamental values—integrity, humility, responsibility, work ethic, entrepreneurship, a thirst for knowledge, the desire to make a contribution, and concern for others—that profoundly influenced the way I do business and live my life to this day. For that, I can never repay my father and mother.

CHAPTER 2

Koch After Fred

BUILDING WITH STONES THAT FIT

Endless human variation ... creates the chance for endless cooperation to the mutual advantage of participants. ... We may reap fruits of human variation and enjoy things not of our own direct creation only if we discover how to allow this cooperation to work.

—BALDY HARPER[1]

Saul Steinberg's *A Parochial New Yorker's View of the World* is an iconic 1975 sketch depicting a Manhattan snob's westward view from Ninth Avenue. (It was the cover art for the *New Yorker* magazine on March 29, 1976, and is still very funny today.)

Before the eye reaches across the Pacific to Japan, China, and Russia, it flits over the American Midwest and West, which appear as Manhattan's modestly sized back lawn—fenced in by Canada and Mexico and sparsely pollinated by tiny insignificant dots: Chicago. Kansas City. Nebraska. Texas. Las Vegas. Los Angeles.

Steinberg's brilliant spoof—meant to highlight a New Yorker's tendency to see other areas as much less significant or distinguishable than they actually are—explains why some people assume Warren Buffett and I have a lot in common. After all, we're each a three-hour drive away from the same speck on the map (Kansas City). Warren and I do happen to know each other, and in addition to running profitable businesses based in Middle America, we both like golf. But that's pretty much where the similarities end. Not only do our political philosophies differ, but so do our business philosophies and companies.

True, Berkshire Hathaway, like Koch, is headquartered in the Midwest and includes an array of seemingly disparate companies. Warren buys companies when their competitive position is attractive, and if their management is good he assures them that he won't intervene except to decide how to invest the cash flow. Then he largely leaves them alone to operate as they had before the acquisition.

Koch's model is different—and has been since the early 1960s when I became involved. Since then, our strategy has been to make acquisitions when we can create additional value by applying our capabilities. This is especially true when the acquisition's capabilities can improve our existing businesses or create new platforms for growth. Both of our largest acquisitions—Georgia-Pacific and Molex—do all of the above.

But make no mistake: While Koch's model for growth today is more systematic than Fred's was, it is still a trial-and-error process. Carefully considered trial is a daily occurrence at Koch. And there have been plenty of errors along the way.

Since 1940, Koch has grown from a start-up to the second largest private U.S. company, not because we happened to be in the right industry at the right time, or because we have friends in high places in Washington, which some critics allege. Instead, Koch has grown through innovation and by painstakingly identifying and acquiring businesses that are beneficial to our customers and Koch as a whole.

I often think of what we do as bricklaying. Or perhaps more precisely, stonemasonry. Once a stone has been carefully selected and set, it shapes a new space in which the mason can set yet another well-chosen stone. Each stone is different, but they all fit together to create a framework that is mutually reinforcing.

While Fred Koch's values were a major influence on me and our Guiding Principles, a capabilities-driven business vision was not part of his thinking. But when he did follow his impulses in directions where we had capabilities, the results were usually excellent: Winkler-Koch, Wood River, Rock Island, and Great Northern.

As I mentioned in the introduction, in the last years of my father's life, his health caused him to become increasingly concerned about the toll that hefty estate taxes would take on the company he had cofounded. What would remain after he passed? Having labored under the "excess profits" tax during World War II, my father knew all too well the feeling of netting next to nothing at the end of the day.

Because of this worry, he resisted capital expenditures, which limited improvements and the addition of more capabilities. Only after we were able to settle my father's estate on a reasonable basis was that constraint lifted, enabling our growth to accelerate.

THE FIRST LAYER OF STONES: CRUDE OIL GATHERING

I was thirty-two when I succeeded my father as chairman and CEO. In the years that followed, Sterling Varner and I focused on increasing the rate of growth of our crude oil gathering business, usually reinvesting 90 percent of the profits as Koch Industries does now. Under Sterling's leadership, Koch grew to become the largest crude purchaser and gatherer in the U.S. and Canada, increasing from 60,000 barrels per day in 1960 to more than 1 million barrels per day in 1990.

This exceptional growth started with a new vision—to become the leading crude oil purchaser by being the most aggressive, providing the best service, and developing the best relationships with crude oil producers. Being aggressive, providing the best service, and developing the best relationships still describe our aspirations today—no matter the business.

Back when Sterling and I began to apply this new vision, most of our customers were independent producers, and our competitors in buying and transporting oil were either small trucking companies or major oil companies. Our vision for winning the independents' business was to be more aggressive and to provide better service at a lower cost than our competitors.

The starting point was soliciting the producers' business as soon as drilling was announced (rather than waiting for the well to succeed). We also had a truck at the site ready to move the oil as soon as the well began producing.

Another capability that gave us an advantage over our small competitors was that we had a balance sheet that (while nothing like those of the majors) gave the producer the confidence that we could always pay for the oil—and pay promptly—even under adverse circumstances. Also we demonstrated we had the organization and systems to pay the right people, even on wells with complex ownership. (Some of these wells had dozens of owners.)

Another key to our growth was developing the capability to build pipelines and to operate pipelines and trucks more economically than our competitors. This was Good Profit 101: providing the best hassle-free service to our clients at the lowest cost to them and attracting the best employees based on the opportunities we offered. Our goal was—and still is—to be the counterparty of choice to our customers, vendors, communities, and employees.

There were certainly times when fate was against us and our investments were unprofitable. But had we been unwilling—or without sufficient capital—to invest, we would have never distinguished ourselves from our competition.

As our crude oil volume grew, at times it was hard to sell it all. So we began to build a crude oil trading capability, enabling us to ensure producers that we could provide a market for their oil—even when there was a surplus. This was the origin of Koch's trading businesses. The next step in our evolution as a "multicompany," which is how *Forbes* magazine classifies us in its annual rankings of private companies, was to begin seeking other opportunities for applying the capabilities we were building in crude oil gathering. This led us into the gas liquids gathering, fractionating, and trading business—and eventually we became the largest such business in the United States. To do so, we had to develop additional capabilities such as handling and storing highly volatile liquids and separating the mixture into purity products.

We then used the capabilities developed in gas liquids to build a natural gas gathering, transporting, processing, and trading business. In turn, our natural gas supply position caused us to pursue forward integration opportunities such as nitrogen fertilizers.

By the early 1970s, Koch had three sets of capabilities that provided us three opportunities to lay the stones to build different structures. They were crude oil gathering, oil refining, and making tower internals—three largely different sets of capabilities.

Once we started, we kept on building. Crude oil gathering enabled us to build businesses in gas liquids and natural gas gathering and processing, and then fertilizers.

Oil refining provided a foundation on which we built a number of other chemical process businesses: chemicals, polymers, fibers, and pulp and paper—some of which took us into consumer products.

The tower internals business positioned us for heat exchangers, burners, flares, membrane separation and other pollution control systems, and gas plant design and construction.

The advent of smart products and smart manufacturing processes for these industries generated our interest in electrical connectors and systems.

Making all this work required having the right people in the right roles. This is something we began to emphasize even before we codified our management system, and it was one of my top priorities upon joining the company. For all his gruffness, my father was actually a very softhearted man who had a tendency to keep people in roles for years that didn't suit them.

Thank goodness Sterling Varner stayed with Koch during its early days, when we had salesmen who drank all day and secretaries who had difficulty typing three lines. Sterling had good sense about these things (and a no-drinking-while-working rule except for a two-drink maximum on evenings when employees were entertaining clients). He also helped get the right people in place in many of our new businesses.

BACK TO REFINING, AND THEN SOME

Don't underestimate the value of the work experience you have as a teenager and young adult. As a teenager I had worked in oilfields over several summers. At Arthur D. Little I had done some consulting work for Exxon (named Standard Oil of New Jersey until 1972).

And for six months in 1962 I worked first as an engineer and then as a salesman at the Great Northern Oil Company's refinery in Minnesota. It was competitively advantaged with a strong market for refined products in Minnesota's Twin Cities. It also benefited from an attractive crude oil supply position, located near Canada's increasing heavy oil production.

Based in part on these early work experiences, I believed we could succeed and grow in refining, and indeed, Koch's 1969 acquisition of controlling interest in the Great Northern Oil Company was the platform that enabled us to enter so many of the businesses that we are in today.

Acquiring GNOC was not a simple, straightforward transaction. It required the application of some of the new concepts I had begun learning, such as entrepreneurship and subjective value, and an even newer one—deal structuring.

After we settled my father's estate taxes, one of my first steps was to approach Union Oil about buying its 40 percent interest in the Great Northern Oil Company. They responded with an offer priced considerably above market, which we declined. They then began trying to sell their interest to independent refining companies, suggesting that prospective buyers could gain control by also acquiring J. Howard Marshall's interest.

To counter this move, I called on J. Howard, who had partnered with us since 1959. I had an idea that only worked because he maintained the same immense trust in me that he had in my late father. I suggested he pool his 15 percent shareholdings with our 35 percent, forming a holding company with controlling interest in GNOC. In the future, I promised, we would exchange J. Howard's interest in the holding company for Koch Industries, Inc., shares, making him a KII shareholder. (Given the quirks of the tax code, had I just offered him KII shares or even agreed on an exchange ratio, it would have made the exchange taxable to him.)

In spite of only having my word that we would make a fair exchange sometime in the future, J. Howard didn't hesitate. He willingly traded his shares in GNOC—for which other buyers would have paid him a control premium—for minority shares in a new Koch subsidiary. Once we owned 50 percent of GNOC, we were able to negotiate Union Oil's shares down to a reasonable price: $25 million.

Such trust is extremely rare in business (or in life), but it paid off for J. Howard in a big way, increasing his net worth many times over as Koch grew. "It turned out to be the best deal I ever made," he later wrote. For Koch Industries it turned out to be a key building block for our extraordinary growth. This transaction vividly illustrates why mutually beneficial voluntary transactions based on trust are the hallmark of economic freedom and vital to good profit.

Great Northern became Koch Refining, and its capabilities enabled other parts of Koch to enter new businesses. Koch Refining (now Flint Hills Resources) has itself become broadly diversified—by entering chemicals, polymers, lubes, and biofuels.

We've acquired seven ethanol plants since 2010, as well as assets and technology to produce other biofuels. Unlike others in the industry, we advocated an end to the government's tax credits for ethanol (which were finally eliminated in 2011), even though we profited from them. And we continue to advocate eliminating the government mandate to use ethanol in gasoline.

Why? Because, as I noted in the introduction, we believe corporate welfare decreases—rather than increases—well-being in society. In any case, by a combination of innovations, we believe we can make our ethanol facilities consistently profitable by economic means instead of political ones. (See chapter 8.)

These new pursuits have not meant the neglect of our refineries. On the contrary, we continue to invest heavily in order to anticipate and meet refining's ever-changing market and environmental conditions. This includes meeting the tightening standards on emissions and energy use and efficiently processing the new supplies of crude oil resulting from shale and oil sands innovations. These have already become a boon to the U.S. and Canadian economies, bringing cheaper and more reliable energy to hundreds of millions of people and substantial good profit to many companies.

Our belief that crude oil from the Canadian oil sands benefits the U.S. economy is why we are in favor of the Keystone Pipeline. Some of our critics allege we will earn a $20 billion profit if the Keystone Pipeline is built, but that is pure fantasy.

We estimate that Keystone would increase the price we pay for Canadian crude by roughly $3 per barrel because it would lower transportation costs to destinations other than our refinery. Recently we have been buying roughly 240,000 barrels per day of Canadian crude to run in our Minnesota refinery. Our Canadian crude oil production has been less than 100 barrels per day. Thus, if Keystone had been in operation it would have lowered Koch Industries' overall profits by $260 million per year.

For the pipeline to make Koch even one dollar more profitable (let alone $20 billion)—rather than less profitable—we would have to increase our Canadian production more than two-thousand-fold—which is far beyond the realm of possibility.

A LAYER OF UNDERSTANDING

In refining, as in all our businesses, developing a superior understanding of our markets has been critical to our approach and to our success. In the 1970s, we began to build world-class market knowledge and quantitative analysis, and to extend our global coverage and physical assets. Having good global intelligence is essential today, given improvements in communications and transportation that make markets global. Since each country has different rules, cultures, and language requiring on-the-ground expertise, operating in a multitude of countries is much more difficult and requires a new set of capabilities.

The quantitative and risk management capabilities we developed for commodity trading helped us build superior capabilities for investing our substantial financial assets and pension funds. This proved invaluable in enabling Koch to preserve capital when the financial crisis hit in 2008.

My brother David exemplifies the importance of shared vision and understanding. Thanks to his leadership and willingness to reinvest profits for continual growth, Koch's process equipment and engineering business has grown over one-thousand-fold since 1961. (My father's faith in David's potential as an engineer was spot-on.)

David joined Koch Engineering in 1970 as a technical services manager and became president of Koch Engineering in 1979. He and his team have greatly expanded and broadened its product lines and capabilities, transforming them into the Koch Chemical Technology Group. KCTG is now a leader in a number of process technology businesses, including mass transfer, combustion, pollution control, heat transfer, membrane separation, and gas plant design and construction. Superior processes and process equipment such as these enable fuels and chemicals to be made more efficiently, with higher purity and less emissions. KCTG's membrane separation systems enable wastewater to be transformed into drinking water, another example of value creation.

AN IMPORTANT EXPERIMENT

Though it might not seem that way to the outside observer, the forest products business has many characteristics in common with oil refining. Not only does wood pulping use chemical processes like oil refining, but both processes can involve a wide variety of raw materials to produce a wide variety of products. Both businesses benefit from having strong engineering, optimization, trading, and logistics capabilities.

Recognizing all this, in 2004 Koch's business development group facilitated the acquisition of a small forest products trading business. After unsuccessfully pursuing a number of other businesses in the field, we learned that Georgia-Pacific was dissatisfied with its stock price, which management believed was depressed because of the perception that GP was a commodity company (despite the fact that nearly half its business was consumer products such as bathroom tissue, paper towels, plates, and cups).

To change that perception, GP had been trying to sell various commodity assets, including two pulp mills. We approached GP's management and succeeded in buying those plants for $610 million in 2004.

We viewed this acquisition as an important experiment. Would our MBM and chemical process industries' capabilities apply to forest products as well? The outcome of this experiment would determine whether forest products should be in Koch's vision going forward. We quickly determined that our purchase of GP's pulp business had been successful when the application of MBM increased both current earnings and future opportunities. Naturally, we then began looking for bigger opportunities in the field.

In 2005, we took a deep breath and made an offer for all of GP—which required taking out the biggest second lien in history at that time. It was a $21 billion acquisition, five times greater than the acquisition involving INVISTA, which was our largest until then.

The additional capabilities and growth platforms that Georgia-Pacific provided Koch in the forest and consumer products industries were quite significant. GP was the world's largest tissue supplier and made many of North America's leading consumer brands, such as Quilted Northern®, Angel Soft®, Brawny®, Sparkle®, and Dixie®. It was also a leader in other segments of the forest products industry—particularly building products and packaging, with prominent brands such as Dens® gypsum products and Plytanium® plywood.

MORE DIVERSIFICATION

Using this same capabilities-driven approach (of always striving to expand and improve the ways we deliver value to customers), our business development team identified the glass industry as an opportunity for us in 2006. This eventually led to our 2012 purchase of a 44.4 percent stake in Guardian Industries. Michigan-based Guardian is a global glass manufacturer that makes the energy-efficient glass used in homes, offices, and skyscrapers; laminated glass for automotive uses; mirrors; and other coated and specialty glass products.

Our second-largest acquisition is Molex, a leading global manufacturer of electronic connectors and other components for smart phones, computers, automobiles, and virtually every other electronic device. Molex strives to identify and satisfy unmet customer needs through rapid innovation and commercialization of new products (including those important to other Koch businesses, such as Georgia-Pacific and Guardian).

Some were surprised by Koch's acquisition of Molex—they

couldn't see the rationale as easily as they could with INVISTA and GP, both of which were in chemical process industries. But to understand where Koch sees opportunity, one needs to remember that we are a capability-driven company. We're convinced that the five dimensions of MBM and Koch's core strengths, such as commercial excellence, can enable Molex to create superior value and help turn it into yet another strong platform for growth. The benefit is mutual. Molex's electronic and IT capabilities can substantially enhance Koch's other products and processes, and business systems.

Today, Koch Industries consists of nine major business groups (see appendix A), a number of minority investments, and the Matador Cattle Company—all of which benefit from MBM and sharing lessons about how to apply it. These businesses also benefit from our six core capabilities in varying degrees (see chapter 6).

This includes our ranching business, which has grown from Fred Koch's original investments to become one of the ten largest cow/calf operations in the United States. Matador Cattle Company specializes in raising Akaushi cattle, a breed created through ninety years of rigorous genetic selection by the Japanese. Akaushi's marbling is much more monounsaturated than others, making it the most heart-healthy. It is also the most tender, delicious beef available.

GRAND PLANS VS.
EXPERIMENTAL DISCOVERY

This brief company history may leave the impression that our experience has been one of ever-improving results, with one success after another, each building on the one before. Nothing could be further from the truth.

Before Koch found a niche with Akaushi beef, our agriculture business went through an "irrational exuberance" phase in the mid-1990s. Our plan was to produce superior steaks to sell at premium prices, revolutionize milling and baking, and become a leader in farm and ranch animal feed through our Purina Mills acquisition.

We talked about capturing the "gas to bread spread"—shorthand for the product chain we thought we could deliver: from natural gas to nitrogen fertilizers to grain to flour . . . to shelf-ready pizza dough.

I mentioned earlier there have been plenty of errors in our trial-and-error approach. A good trial-and-error approach would test the validity of such a large-scale venture before plunging headfirst. The size of the experiment should have been limited in proportion to the risk-adjusted potential of the opportunity.

We neglected to apply this experimental discovery model to our "gas to bread spread" theory, and suffered sizeable losses as a result. And in a cruel twist of irony, our unsold pizza dough inventory was fed to the ranch animals.

The point is that progress—whether in business, an economy, or science—comes through experimentation and failure. Those who favor a "grand plan" over experimentation fail to understand the role that failed experiments play in creating progress in society. Failures quickly and efficiently signal what doesn't work, minimizing waste and redirecting scarce resources to what does work. A market economy is an experimental discovery process, in which business failures are inevitable and any attempt to eliminate them only ensures even greater failures.

For experimental discovery to work, we have to not only design experiments properly but also *recognize* when we are experimenting so we can limit the bet accordingly. Koch companies have suffered whenever we forgot we were experimenting and made bets as if the risks were small when they were not.

One of our worst such bets involved overblown petroleum and tanker trading positions in the early 1970s. During the OPEC crisis of 1973–74, we were caught with positions beyond our capability to handle, leaving us with large losses as the Arab countries held back their oil supply, causing the tanker market to collapse.

That was certainly a great learning experience, but I'm not sure I could stand that much learning again.

I would like to say these were Koch's only business failures, but there have been plenty of others (see appendix B). Ironically, a key factor in our success has been the willingness to admit to such mistakes and mitigate our losses in a timely manner. Rather than squandering our scarcest resource (talent) trying to save a marginal business, we've learned to focus that resource on opportunities with real potential.

To put all this in perspective, here's a sobering thought: The losses from all our bad deals combined are less than the gains we missed out on from just one of the major opportunities we failed to capture. These include oil refineries, oil reserves, fertilizer companies, and chemical companies, any one of which would have generated profits in excess of these losses if we had bought it at the right time.

Please note, however, that many of the businesses we've sold or exited were not failures. They were successes, but then they reached a point in their life cycle where we believed we could no longer create sufficient value with them. As such, they became more valuable to someone else.

Given the differences in each company's capabilities and circumstances, the value of any given business or plant will vary greatly from one company to another. Everyone has reasons for valuing one product, service, or opportunity over another. Our practice of exiting businesses with limited potential for us and focusing on ones with greater potential has been a key element in our success.

"The stone the builders rejected has become the cornerstone" is a Bible verse with resonance for Koch, considering all the stones we have selected as we've grown. Some have fit us; some haven't. (But that doesn't mean they won't become the cornerstone of someone else's building.)

With each stone we choose, the shape of the next one becomes apparent.

CHAPTER 3

Queens, Factory Girls, and Schumpeter

THE INCREDIBLE (SOMETIMES TERRIFYING) BENEFITS OF CREATIVE DESTRUCTION

The capitalist achievement does not typically consist in providing more silk stockings for queens, but in bringing them within reach of factory girls in return for steadily decreasing amounts of effort.

—JOSEPH SCHUMPETER[1]

My wife, Liz, jokes that she knew when we were married in 1972 she would have an interesting life. But she didn't realize there would be moments of *sheer terror.*

One of those moments came not long after we married. We were living in my cramped bachelor apartment—overflowing with books, where I had settled after moving back to Wichita from Boston. Since Koch headquarters was in Wichita, where we were both born and raised, Liz and I intended to put down roots and raise our family here. (Elizabeth was born in 1975, followed by Chase in 1977.)

In 1974, we broke ground on what would be our first home—just as Koch Industries was experiencing some of its darkest hours as a company. The Arab oil crisis, occurring simultaneously with U.S. wage and price controls, dealt the company a vicious one-two punch. I was very worried it could bankrupt us.

One night I sat at the edge of our home's freshly dug foundation, with my feet dangling in the hole, contemplating the big mistake we might be making. I was worried that if the company went under, this house would take me under as well. "Well," I said to Liz, "it's not too late. We can just cancel the rest of the construction and fill in this hole."

Despite some painful lessons, both the company and the hole managed to survive. In fact, we still live in that house today. (Admittedly, it has been redecorated a few times since the 1970s, but never remodeled.) Even though things worked out in the end, that experience taught me what a potentially life-changing loss can do to one's nerves.

Liz understands this, too. Her grandfather, Allen Hinkel, went to work for the Wallenstein & Cohn Boston Store, eventually acquiring full ownership of it by 1924. He renamed it Hinkel's department store, and it had fourteen locations throughout the American Southwest at its peak. Liz began working retail in Hinkel's two Wichita-area stores when she was thirteen. By age twenty-two, she had worked her way up to the position of the misses and juniors separates buyer, a role that involved a great deal of business acumen and responsibility—which she quickly embraced. She has only become savvier with age.

In the 1970s, most family-owned department stores went the way of the dinosaur as customers chose discounted chain merchandisers like Kmart over mom-and-pop stores like Hinkel's, whose personalized customer service came at the expense of higher prices. At the other end of the retail spectrum, smaller specialized shops (with fewer overhead costs) successfully competed against large department stores like Hinkel's—another development that put many out of business.

Then came the lost interest income previously generated by Hinkel's store-issued charge cards once consumers began using American Express, Visa, and Mastercard to make their purchases. To make matters even worse, Hinkel's had to pay transaction fees to banks on those card purchases (often as high as 5 percent), so its net gain from charge cards turned into a net loss. That pretty much finished off Hinkel's and countless family-owned department stores like it, long before the Internet threatened brick-and-mortar retailers with creative destruction.

Successful businesspeople stand on ground that is "crumbling beneath their feet,"[2] said Joseph Schumpeter, who taught at Harvard in the 1930s and '40s and is one of the most important economists of the twentieth century. His observation about the tenuousness of success is a tough fact every established business faces.

At Koch, we've known for a long time that there is no getting around this reality. As Adam Smith noted three centuries ago, many people have tried to protect their businesses through political means—but always to the detriment of society as a whole. Rather than following this practice, Koch strives to drive what Schumpeter called *creative destruction*, creating "the new commodity, the new technology, the new source of supply, the new type of organization."[3]

In 2014, Liz and I enjoyed a once-in-a-lifetime trip to France with our kids and grandsons to celebrate her seventieth birthday. We found much to admire while we were there, but I shook my head at the new French law intended to keep small, independent bookstores profitable by prohibiting the free delivery of discounted books from online retailers.

I am a bona fide book person. My home contains more books than I'll ever have time to count, and the walls of my Wichita office are lined with them, too. But as much as I love books, I believe coercing people to patronize small bookshops is disrespectful to French consumers. Moreover, it ignores the reality that the ground is crumbling beneath the old model of bookselling.

The role of business is to respect and satisfy what customers value (even if it's other forms of merchandising) rather than lobbying the government to mandate what can or cannot be offered. Such activities are the ultimate form of disrespect for customers. In a society that maximizes people's well-being, business would only profit if it is doing a good job listening and responding to changing needs and wants.

When companies do that well, business benefits and so does society. But to do so requires a deep acceptance and understanding of the fact that consumer needs and desires are constantly evolving.

What this means, for example, is that mainframes will be replaced by personal computers, if customers are respected. Granted, this may feel terrible if you are a mainframe computer manufacturer—or a small bookstore owner, or an oil refiner facing shrinking gasoline demand, for that matter. But this only reinforces the importance of being attuned to your customers' changing desires, anticipating them, and building the capability to satisfy them when you are able to do so.

There is no way around the conditions necessary for generating good profit. The system must allow those who do the best job of satisfying customers to succeed; only then will both companies and consumers benefit. "The . . . process of industrial mutation . . . incessantly revolutionizes the economic structure from within, incessantly destroying the old one, incessantly creating a new one. This process of creative destruction is the essential fact of capitalism,"[4] Schumpeter wrote.

Over the long term, Schumpeter's concept of creative destruction benefits almost everyone who lives in a society that allows it—even if it doesn't appear immediately evident to the owners or employees of a business whose ground has crumbled beneath them.

When a business succeeds through creative destruction, a chain reaction ripples through a whole variety of businesses and communities, hurting some and helping others—but on the whole, making people in society better off.

LOGIC VS. FEELINGS

Growing up, I saw how both of my parents were deeply concerned about people, but in different ways. My mother placed great emphasis on other people's needs and felt a deep sense of obligation to everyone she knew. She was a very sensitive woman. To my way of thinking, she took her focus on others to such an extreme that it was sometimes to her detriment. She felt guilty turning down invitations or requests from people she cared about, even if it meant having to be in four places at the same time.

In many ways, my mother was a perfect counterbalance for my father, whose concern (especially about the spread of Communism) was more impersonal. "This technical work does not tend to make a very human individual out of a person," he admitted in a letter to one of his friends.[5]

Like my father, I have a mathematical, logic-driven mind and am thankfully balanced out by my people-focused, intuitive wife. (Don't let my Bergamo story lead you to believe I don't love Italians. Liz's maiden name is Buzzi, and I have been the beneficiary of her warmth and loyalty ever since we met forty-eight years ago.)

This tension between logic and feelings—ever-present in creative destruction—has long intrigued me. I remember a lengthy and heated debate over political philosophy I had with my brother David's New York girlfriend in the late 1960s. As we argued, she took increasingly extreme positions on the extent to which government should run people's lives—for the alleged good of the majority, as she interpreted it.

Finally I asked her whether she believed in the protections for individual rights provided in our constitutional form of government. She responded that she didn't. The government, she argued, should be free to act however the majority wanted.

I challenged her: "If you were a redhead, you would be okay if the majority voted to kill all the redheads?" This shut down her aggressive argument and made her cry. Her foundational belief system was so shattered that she was still crying the next morning.

Her reaction made such a deep impression on me that I still think about it five decades later. It helped me understand what it takes to get people to come to grips with deeply held beliefs based not on facts and logic, but on feelings. It may not feel comfortable to some, but if the goal is providing the factory girl the same silk stockings worn by Prince William's wife, Kate Middleton (or the even better stockings made from our nylon or LYCRA®), then logic—and history—tells us that market-driven creative destruction is much better than government limiting progress by protecting established businesses.

Of course, the downside is the discomfort of knowing the same girl's factory job might not exist next year if her employers succumb to creative destruction. That consideration is no small thing.

I won't pretend this doesn't cause the factory girl stress—or even sheer terror. But of this I am certain: Her standard of living will be many times higher in a society that allows constructive change than in a society that doesn't—because the rate of innovation and the level of productivity will be so much higher.

Value creation is the upside of creative destruction. It makes people's lives better, thereby contributing to well-being in society. A successful company creates value by providing products or services customers value more highly than their alternatives, such as less-expensive books delivered to their homes versus more-expensive books shelved in small shops. A successful business doesn't earn good profit by attempting to force customers to buy its books at independent bookshops. That is bad profit.

Good profit comes from responding to customers who volunteer their dollars to have books delivered to their homes by a faceless website and its algorithms—or to purchase them in a big box store that sells many other items besides books.

Again, responding to customers is the proper role of business in society. The once-popular BlackBerry became unprofitable because, although efficient for direct communication, it has far fewer apps, which makes Internet access harder than with an iPhone. Old steel mills lost out to more efficient mini-mills that processed scrap instead of iron ore. Service stations were replaced by convenience stores. In every case, consumers became better off.

When an unprofitable business is supported by subsidies or protected by political means (like the French book-shipping law), it is not using resources efficiently. Losses indicate that consumers more highly value other uses for those resources. The wasteful use of resources, when repeated throughout society, seriously erodes well-being. Artificially propping up businesses is bad for consumers, and ultimately bad for the employees of those businesses, since change is inevitable. Businesses that are not allowed to experience natural disruption often are subject to much more severe shocks and more difficult adjustments. Many people in places like Detroit know this all too well. Employees of businesses that do not evolve will soon be out of a job.

When developing Market-Based Management, I didn't rely on the thinkers and societies that condemn people to lifetimes of poverty, dependency, and hopelessness. Instead, MBM draws from the wisdom of philosophers, economists, and psychologists willing to face reality and use logic—accepting the periodic feelings of sheer terror that accompany it.

ECONOMIC FREEDOM AS A CONDITION FOR CREATIVE DESTRUCTION

Because organizations are miniature societies, MBM, when properly implemented, achieves the same positive outcomes as free national economies that generate widespread well-being and opportunity. Free societies generate these benefits even when they don't have great natural endowments. Hong Kong and Singapore, for example, were not blessed with abundant natural resources, but their standard of living is among the highest in the world.

While it's true they don't have the same level of social and political freedom as New Zealand or Switzerland, they do offer people the greatest economic freedom compared to all the other countries in the world—and thus some of the greatest opportunities.

The Fraser Institute's Economic Freedom of the World Index takes into account many factors that affect the ability of people in a particular country to choose how they work, produce, consume, and invest. Those factors include property rights, free trade, sound money, and harmful regulation.[6]

Greater economic freedom is strongly correlated with not only higher income per capita, but with longer life expectancy, better environmental quality, improved health and education, less corruption, and better living standards—especially for the poor.

Empirical study should lead one to conclude that long-term, widespread well-being is much more likely in free societies. By the same token, examples of prosperity in unfree societies—based on such things as superior natural resources—are few and far be-

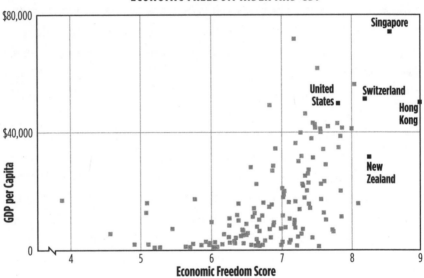

ECONOMIC FREEDOM INDEX AND GDP

Data courtesy of the Fraser Institute's Economic Freedom of the World: 2014 Annual Report.[7]

tween, and generally short-lived. Life for the overwhelming majority of people who haven't been blessed to live in a free society has been, as Hobbes put it, "poor, nasty, brutish, and short."[8]

Businesses can create much more well-being in free societies that are ordered through voluntary cooperation and competition than in unfree societies that are ordered through government mandates. In a society with rules of just conduct, in order to benefit ourselves we must benefit others. Adam Smith summed up this process when he wrote, "It is not from the benevolence of the butcher, the brewer, or the baker that we expect our dinner, but from their regard to their own interest."[9]

Self-interest is often confused with selfishness or self-absorption in modern dictionaries and textbooks. Alexis de Tocqueville's respect is evident for the enlightened self-interest he observed in the American economy of the 1800s, as he watched people benefit themselves by benefiting others: "Americans . . . are fond of explaining almost all actions of their lives by the principle of self-interest rightly understood; they show with complacency how an enlightened regard for themselves constantly prompts them to assist one another."[10]

It is not a question of whether or not there should be self-interest, because the opposite of self-interest is extinction. The essential question is how to channel that self-interest for the general good. "No individual could survive in a world of scarce resources without a strong measure of self-interest, one that includes at the very least his own family and close associates," wrote noted law professor and prolific author Richard Epstein.[11] "That self-interest can manifest itself in one of two ways when dealing with strangers; through either aggression or cooperation."

Whether in civil society or in business, mutual benefit is achieved only when rules are in place to make sure people don't use aggression (force or deceit) to advance their self-interest. According to Nobel Prize–winning economist Vernon Smith, these "beneficial rules of exchange" are "the right of possession, its transference by consent, and the performance of promises."[12] This system encourages profiting by economic means, not political means. Businesses that don't create value by economic means are undermining well-being for all.

Political economist Franz Oppenheimer clearly distinguished these "two fundamentally opposed means"[13] by which people obtain resources to satisfy their desires. The economic means of profiting involves voluntarily exchanging your goods or services with others for money. Parties will not voluntarily enter into an exchange unless both believe they will be better off. Therefore, you can only profit over time in a system of voluntary exchange (a market) by making others better off.

The political means of profiting transfers goods, services, or money from one party to another by force or fraud—for example, by laws or regulations that redirect consumer choices or that violate Vernon Smith's rules of exchange and fail to hold accountable those who don't fulfill their side of a contract.

When all of us act out of self-interest, governed by beneficial rules of exchange, value is created by economic means. This results in the harmonious system, not ordained by government, that Hayek described as "spontaneous order" in society. In the 1940s, Hungarian-born polymath Michael Polanyi, who ranks with Karl Popper as one of the greatest philosophers of science, found that organizations have their own spontaneous order—and it is this order that is so beneficial to creating value in society.

Polanyi's spontaneous order is what the union leader near Bergamo thought was too radical to implement in Italy. "Workers work, managers think," is a command-and-control approach, and command-and-control companies are less innovative and less competitive over time. Such companies have a much harder time making silk stockings that are affordable for factory girls than the companies that do so through beneficial incentives and generalized rules of conduct.

Smith and Hayek demonstrated that prosperity can take place only through spontaneous order, an order that results from unscripted human action, not human design. Smith described this as the "invisible hand" by which, in the proper system, man is led "to promote an end which is no part of his intentions."[14] Hayek showed how prosperity requires that the knowledge dispersed throughout society be put to productive use, saying it "cannot be gathered and conveyed to an authority charged with the task of deliberately creating order."[15]

This point was memorably illustrated by economist Thomas Sowell in his book *Knowledge and Decisions*: "When Soviet nail factories had their output measured by weight, they tended to make big, heavy nails, even if those big nails sat unsold on the shelves while the country was crying out for small nails."[16] In other words, when governments plan how people should run their lives, everybody (but those in power) loses.

But when people and companies are free to innovate using their knowledge of what they and others value, consumers benefit, enabling business to generate good profit.

Only spontaneous order, resulting from unscripted human action, can answer the demand of people who need nails. By harnessing the principles of free societies—which generate knowledge obtained from prices and profits and loss—organizations benefit tremendously. The knowledge obtained by understanding the drivers of profits and losses enables an organization to determine the number and types of nails needed.

Replicating the way the scientific community organizes itself, wherein knowledge is shared freely with a commitment to disproving even the most cherished hypotheses, leads to innovation. Likewise, it provides powerful benefits for organizations. Polanyi makes this parallel, comparing the scientific community to business in his 1962 paper "The Republic of Science":

> The community of scientists is organized in a way which resembles certain features of a body politic and works according to economic principles similar to those by which the production of material goods is regulated. Much of what I will have to say will be common knowledge among scientists, but I believe that it will recast the subject from a novel point of view which can both profit from and have a lesson for political and economic theory.[17]

Certainly Koch has benefited from the theories espoused in Polanyi's "The Republic of Science." (I used the methodology he described to write this book, soliciting input from knowledgeable sources throughout Koch.) We are able to create superior value for customers because we attempt to replicate a free community of scientists—constantly sharing knowledge and ideas, testing hypotheses, experimenting and adjusting according to what honestly works—rather than succumbing to establishmentarian pressures.

People used to think the sun revolved around the Earth because it fit their notion that everything ought to revolve around the Earth. Humans lived on Earth, after all. Thus they had a "mental model" that wrongly assumed the Earth was the center of the universe. The consequences of this faulty model delayed scientific advancements, and even landed a dissenting physicist—Galileo—under house arrest for daring to challenge religious dogma enforced by government.

Mental models are intellectual structures that enable us to simplify and organize the myriad inputs we get from the world around us. They shape and support our thinking, decision making, opinions, values, and beliefs. Ludwig von Mises said of mental models, "They are a necessary requirement of any intellectual grasp of historical events."[18]

Yet Buddha warned us not to believe anything just because it is commonly accepted, or even on the authority of our teachers but only when, "after observation and analysis, when it agrees with reason, and is conducive to the good and gain of one and all."[19]

The quality of our mental models determines how well we function in the physical world. The same is true for the economic world, which is why Koch Industries invests tremendous time and effort to ensure that our MBM mental models fit reality. Any business with behavior based on faulty mental models will eventually fail. We must constantly remind ourselves that just because we believe or want a thing to be true does not make it so.

The most reliable signal that a business is using reality-grounded mental models and providing service that customers truly value is a profit made over time under beneficial rules of just conduct. Short-term profit, created by liquidating assets and avoiding expenditures necessary for long-term success, can be illusory. (The opportunity for us to buy Chrysler Realty presented itself in 1979 because Chrysler, which had been showing "profits," was actually on the verge of bankruptcy due to its failure to make necessary investments.)

When one of our businesses is profitable in the long term, we have some confidence that we are achieving our goal of creating value by helping people improve their lives, and doing a superior job of using resources more efficiently than our competitors.

Consuming as few resources as possible while creating value for customers leaves more resources available to satisfy other needs in society. Long-term profitability indicates that the resources consumed have a higher value in that use than in alternate uses— customers are voting for one use over another with their dollars.

An entrepreneur's resources are not just capital, raw materials, and energy. They also include knowledge, labor, time, and other inputs. Superior value can be created by converting these resources into a product or service that has greater value to the customer than its alternatives, or by consuming fewer or lower-cost resources to provide the same product or service.

For example, more value is created by making fabric with LYCRA than with commodity spandex. Producers of fabric are able to run their production lines faster because the LYCRA fiber breaks less. It also lasts longer and recovers better after stretching than does commodity spandex. When gasoline is made by a more energy-efficient process, or in a way that produces a higher yield, the resulting product may be the same, but resources are conserved. While we often tend to focus on the direct benefits we can see, like cheaper goods for consumers, the "unseen" benefits to society as a whole can be even greater over time.

Koch companies turn crude oil into products such as fuels and asphalt, and polymers into fibers for carpets and clothes. If we can make these products using fewer or less-costly raw materials, several good things happen. The resources saved are available to satisfy other needs, enabling people throughout society to benefit from lower prices while allowing Koch to earn good profits. We reinvest these profits to create new products enabling us to hire and reward employees.

In a free market with property rights and beneficial rules of conduct, profitability through voluntary transactions is not a signal that one party is taking advantage of another. Quite the contrary, "good" profitability is the appropriate measure of an enterprise's contribution to society.

That is why a business that continues to be unprofitable should be restructured, sold to a better-suited owner, or shut down. If a business requires subsidies or protective laws to survive or employ more people, it is not generating good profit. Although I do not want to minimize the stress and fear that often accompany loss of employment, virtually everyone would be better off if those people were employed where they could be more productive.

Change is ever-present in society, the economy, and politics. Companies, products, methods, and individual skills are constantly being replaced by superior alternatives. By relentlessly applying a business philosophy that seeks rather than runs from these alternatives, all of us at Koch have worked hard to counter the tendency toward long-term decline of those who don't innovate.

Companies must realize they are not competing just on price and output of existing products. They have to relentlessly strive to come up with new and better products and produce them more efficiently than the alternatives. They also need to constantly improve the way they're organized, so they can innovate and eliminate waste better than their competitors. This is what MBM enables Koch to do—and it is what MBM can enable you to do, as well.

Schumpeter's observation bears repeating: "It is not [price and output] competition which counts, but the competition from the new commodity, the new technology, the new source of supply, the new type of organization—competition which commands a decisive cost or quality advantage and which strikes not at the margins of the profits and the outputs of the existing firms but at their foundations and their very lives."[20]

Our attempt to heed Schumpeter is why lower prices or better supply isn't all we offer customers. It's why we continuously offer new products, such as INVISTA's Raptor™ nylon pipe for oilfield gathering systems, which can replace steel and other materials, is corrosion resistant, and is cheaper and easier to install. It's why we continue to develop new technologies, such as bioprocesses to make industrial chemicals. It's why we arrange new sources of supply, such as bringing crude oil from the growing Eagle Ford field to our Corpus Christi refinery. And it's why we have developed MBM, with an aim to become a new type of organization that is the counterparty of choice for every customer, vendor, employee, and community.

MBM teaches that we must continually drive constructive change in every aspect of our company or we will fail. As a result, we constantly pursue disruptive innovations and opportunities through internal and external development as well as acquisition. Similarly, we shed businesses and assets that are unprofitable or worth more to others. We believe we must drive creative destruction faster than our competitors; otherwise it will drive us out of business.

Every business is vulnerable to creative destruction, but MBM can enable the company to drive it rather than succumb. Koch's reality-grounded MBM mental models, customer focus, and innovation have made us one of the world's largest and most successful private companies, generating exceptional long-term performance.

While our workforce has grown by more than 70,000 over the past decade, there have also been some shutdowns and restructurings. In order to be competitive, we reluctantly make these decisions. But there is a flip side to this coin: when these decisions enable us to create more value, we can employ more people in the long term. We also try to find opportunities for affected employees with the right virtues in other parts of Koch and, if that's not possible, elsewhere in the business community.

Even successful companies struggle to keep up because, given human nature, we all tend to become complacent, self-protective, and less innovative as we succeed. It can be far more difficult to overcome success than adversity. I mentioned in the previous chapter that this was a lesson my father impressed on me at an early age: "Often adversity is a blessing in disguise and is certainly the greatest character builder."

Fred Koch's reminder that I didn't know as much as I thought I did helped open my eyes and (ideally) guides my thinking at Koch Industries to this day. We can't tell the customer what he should value—but we can suggest a better way to satisfy him. Most innovations are driven by competing suppliers suggesting better ways for customers to satisfy their needs. Because IBM was so invested in mainframes, it didn't lead the personal computer and Internet revolutions. As a result, IBM was the victim of creative destruction driven by its competitors. The same is true for Kodak, which invented digital photography.

If you want to generate good profit in your organization, you have to constantly strive to discover, respect, and satisfy what customers value, and even anticipate what they will value in the future. The ground is always crumbling beneath our feet. The good news is, Schumpeter was right: Nowadays, factory girls have access to the same silk stockings as queens.

CHAPTER 4

Overcoming Bureaucracy and Stagnation

ECONOMIC CONCEPTS TO SET YOU FREE

The man who grasps principles can successfully select his own methods. The man who tries methods, ignoring principles, is sure to have trouble.

—RALPH WALDO EMERSON (ATTRIBUTED)[1]

One day in the early 1980s, I was sitting in the office of a vice president at a major oil company, listening with dismay to his tales of corporate woe: bureaucracy, resistance to change, red tape, and so forth. It sounded nightmarish to me. "How in the world does someone survive here?" I asked him.

"After a while you just paint your a** white and run with the antelope!" he confided.

I chuckled at the depiction of his sad reality—that his own organization was stagnating and there was nothing he could do about it, so he had to give up. In truth, this is really no laughing matter. There's a tendency for many in successful companies to rest on their laurels and become complacent, self-protective, and less innovative. In such bureaucratic cultures, employees can survive only by running with the herd. Decline sets in.

Having witnessed plenty of complacency in companies during

my time consulting at Arthur D. Little, I could never bear to see Koch stagnating. From very early on at the company, I've wanted to prevent that by creating the same conditions inside Koch that lead to long-term prosperity in society. Guided by the similarities between societies and organizations, I introduced basic economic concepts such as opportunity cost, subjective value, and comparative advantage.

These concepts were often taught in economics departments and business schools, but they were rarely applied in the schools themselves, or in most businesses. Everywhere I looked—including inside Koch—people were often making decisions ignoring basic economic concepts.

One day, for example, our crude oil supply team was considering when we should sell some crude oil inventory. They wanted to wait, rather than sell immediately, betting that the price would rise above their cost.

I challenged them. Sunk costs—such as the price we had already paid for that inventory—should not govern decisions. Instead, decisions need to be driven by forward-looking analysis. The only argument for waiting longer to sell the inventory would be if, on balance, the evidence indicated the price was likely to rise rather than fall further, or even stay the same.

A sunk cost (or "book" cost) is an unrecoverable past expenditure. In general, such costs should not be taken into account when determining what to do in the future because, other than possible tax effects, they are irrelevant to what can be recovered.

The true cost of any activity is the highest-value activity forgone—that is, the opportunity cost. This is the methodology I encourage employees to use in making decisions, and I strive to practice what I preach.

For example, while writing this book, grammatical questions often tempted me to stop and consult my well-worn copy of "Strunk & White." Since a team of professional editors at Crown would eventually scrub these pages, any time I spent in "Strunk & White" would have had too high an opportunity cost to justify. I would have had to forgo actually writing this book (and contributing to Koch) in those minutes spent working on grammar.

I understand why employees everywhere commit this error, even when they understand the theory. One reason is that their incentives are improperly structured. When employees are rewarded only for short-term accounting profits without factoring in what long-term profits were missed, they will tend to make suboptimal decisions. To counter this, Koch treats a portion of the potential profit from a missed opportunity as an actual loss when determining an employee's incentive compensation.

At Koch we also urge our salespeople to *understand each customer's subjective values and tailor the way we deal with them accordingly.* Many public companies value steady, predictable earnings more than larger (on average) earnings that are more volatile, since steady earnings tend to result in a higher stock price. Because of this difference in subjective values between us and our customers, it can be mutually beneficial for us to absorb the price risk in our contracts, and for them to compensate us for it.

So, if one of our ethylene customers wants fixed margins to avoid volatility, we'll agree to absorb the price fluctuations between the ethylene we're selling them and the plastic they're making with it. For us to be willing to do that, we must believe we're being adequately compensated for the risk. Koch is always willing to do this kind of win-win business.

Our application of comparative advantage, a different concept, has led to major changes in the way we fill various roles. What this concept says is that each person—and each organization and even each nation, for that matter—can compete and make a contribution, even if others can do everything better. No nation, organization, or individual should attempt to do everything, no matter how good they are. The reason comes down to comparative advantage.

Imagine a talented consultant opens his own shop. Not only is this consultant a highly valued advisor to his clients; he's also an office-managing dynamo—great at billing, IT, database organization, making his own travel arrangements, and so on. He can run his office better than anyone else he could pay to do it, and on top of that, he's a spectacular cleaner, too. He can clean the office complex far better than anyone he could hire to do it.

So should he keep his costs low by not hiring an office manager and janitor, filling both roles himself? A frugal person might instinctively answer "yes," but the math shows otherwise. Imagine he would need to pay an office manager $1,000 a week for a forty-hour workweek, and a janitor $20 an hour, ten hours a week. If he managed and cleaned his own office, he would save $1,200 a week.

But even if this consultant is twice as efficient as any office manager or janitor, he would still need to spend twenty-five hours a week on activities other than consulting (twenty hours managing and five hours cleaning). If he bills consulting clients $500 an hour, this would create a $12,500 (25 × $500) opportunity cost (i.e., the cost in revenue he could have generated had he not been managing the office and cleaning) against a savings of $1,200 a week. That's a net loss of $11,300 a week. Clearly his comparative advantage is consulting—not cleaning or office managing.

Once we understood how this concept enhances prosperity through the division of labor and trade, we began designing roles for employees not only according to what best fit their capabilities, but *in relation to the roles and capabilities of other employees.* Given the uniqueness of each individual, this application requires a continual reassessment of roles and responsibilities.

Let's say Koch lost Sue, a sales manager who was good at strategy, and then hired Peg, who had good customer relations skills but was not good at strategy. Unless we tailored Peg's role accordingly, her performance would suffer.

We should ask Peg to focus on her advantage: customer relations. In fact, we would give Peg expanded customer relations responsibility, and assign the strategic duties to another strategy-savvy person from inside the company, if we had that skill available.

When people change roles in other companies, too often their replacements are expected to take on the exact same roles and responsibilities, despite having different strengths and weaknesses. In such an environment, comparative advantages are no longer optimized, opportunity costs are excessive, and the performance of the group suffers.

Back in the 1970s, we were small enough that these market concepts could be infused informally throughout the company's leadership. In meetings, I would mentor our people by asking relevant questions, such as "Have we considered the opportunity cost?" or "What are the comparative advantages?" Productivity and performance began to rise.

An essential concept for us is *competitive* advantage (the ability of a business to create greater value than its competitors), which is different than comparative advantage. This is a key building block in our Decision Making Framework used to analyze investment-making opportunities (see chapter 9).

As Koch continued to grow, our knowledge and talent pool were becoming increasingly large and dispersed, which meant I was only able to coach a small percentage of our employees in concepts such as these. Consequently, our ability to apply them to achieve results was diminishing, even as our opportunity to benefit from them was increasing as Koch expanded. We needed to find ways to teach the theory and practice of our concepts and mental models on a much larger scale.

So even before I officially launched MBM inside Koch, I sought to incorporate the values, economic thinking, philosophy, psychological concepts, mental models, and resulting tools, such as those just described, into an existing management system.

It was the early 1980s when I selected W. Edwards Deming's system for this melding. It appealed to me because Deming used statistical methods to improve quality and emphasized continuous improvement in a company. (And, as I mentioned before, I passionately disliked the idea of our employees running with the antelope.)

Deming was a Yale-educated statistician who achieved worldwide fame after he was brought to Japan in 1947 by Gen. Douglas MacArthur to resuscitate industry and manufacturing after World

War II. It worked. In 1960, Emperor Hirohito awarded Deming Japan's Second Order Medal of the Sacred Treasure for engineering the country's industrial rebirth and worldwide success.

Deming emphasized a company's need to keep improving and innovating—or face extinction. "You never get out of this hospital," he warned.[2] Deming's approach helped us systematize continuous improvement, which was an important early aspect of Market-Based Management.

Under Deming, we used Pareto charts, root cause analysis, and statistical process control to better identify and solve problems, and to measure our progress in clear and meaningful ways. Some of it helped. But another important lesson I learned during this period was not from Deming himself. It was from a visit to our gas liquids plant in Medford, Oklahoma.

During the visit I stopped by the plant's electrical shop. Because of my arrival, the electricians were all busying themselves drawing control charts (everyone in the company was aware of my belief in the usefulness of control charts) instead of doing electrical work. To my dismay, I learned that they referred to this exercise as "charts for Charles." (A certain amount of mockery comes with the CEO job. The joke among our employees in the oilfields was that Koch stood for "Keep Ol' Charlie Happy.")

At Medford, measurement and chart drawing had become the focus rather than improving performance and eliminating waste. Apparently we hadn't made clear that charts or measurements of activity were not an end in themselves; their purpose was to improve results.

Ultimately, the charts for Charles incident took us in a much better direction. It became obvious that we could not simply graft our principles and mental models onto an existing management system, even one as good as Deming's. We needed to develop our own framework, one that would help turn our concepts into effective problem-solving tools.

Koch is now a huge company that encompasses many businesses

and straddles several industries. We can't squander resources by having our valuable talent applying continuous improvement to something that will create $100,000 in value when they can make a more radical improvement that could create $10 million in value.

That's why we replaced Deming's continuous improvement with Schumpeter's creative destruction. Creative destruction was more fundamental and more substantive. Continuous improvement, while beneficial, could mean just making modest incremental improvements to something that is becoming obsolete.

Creative destruction involves finding new and better ways, making old ways obsolete. That's a much better fit for Koch—or any company that wants to maximize value and growth.

While our engagement with Deming didn't result in a management marriage, it was actually quite beneficial in ways we never expected. It led us to systematically articulate our own framework based on theory and practice. We now know that a coherent framework of five dimensions that are mutually reinforcing, like four walls and a ceiling, creates far greater benefits than five non-intersecting planes.

In 1990, as we began codifying our system into its five dimensions, I came up with the name Market-Based Management. I felt it reflected the influence of market principles and the need to provide a coherent management philosophy and practice. The initial challenge was to discover or develop the mechanisms that would enable us to truly harness the power of a market economy within the company.

To that end, we established the MBM Development Group. This group had no products or services to sell. Its main purpose was to develop tools for the organization from market principles. Teams were formed to study how organizations can capture the power of property rights, rules of just conduct, values, culture, vision, measurement, incentives, profit and loss, and prices. We went so far as having professors lecture us on theory. Candidly, much of this turned out not to be very useful.

Early on, I had a faulty mental model about who understood MBM—or even what true understanding was. I confused articulate conceptual knowledge with knowledge of how to apply the concepts to get results. In other words, the team we assembled was much better at articulating the concepts than practicing them.

Polanyi argued that we only truly know something—that is, have personal knowledge of it—when we can apply it to get results. As I mentioned earlier, knowing the theory of the golf swing and shooting a low score are two different things.

This is consistent with what I've observed among oil explorers: There are those who can beautifully articulate the technicalities of underground formations and reservoirs but never manage to find oil. On the other hand, there are those who aren't fluent in explaining why or how but are very good at finding oil.

Polanyi's articulation of the difference between personal knowledge and conceptual knowledge put this in perspective and helped us accelerate our progress in the development and application of MBM. Theoretical grounding is necessary, but by itself it is not sufficient to obtain results. Success in applying new mental models— and thus acquiring personal knowledge—comes only after correct, frequent, and prolonged practice. Practice makes permanent (not perfect); thus it has to be done correctly.

Besides, our primary need at that point was not more conceptual knowledge of the underlying theory; it was better personal knowledge of how to apply it to generate good profit. As Cambridge professor Mary Beard observed: "Action without study is fatal. Study without action is futile."[3]

During the era of the MBM Development Group, concepts became little more than buzzwords used by employees to justify what they were already doing—or worse, what they wanted to do. For example, someone operating a process unit at a plant might take MBM's respect for "local knowledge" and use it as an excuse to ignore any help offered from headquarters in Wichita. That's a misapplication of local knowledge.

A process unit operator might know how to optimize the unit

on a given day, but is he aware of the improvements being developed around the world, including those from other industries? He might know how to run that unit more efficiently than anyone else, but is he up-to-date on best practices and all the latest environmental and safety rules? Overcoming similar misapplications of concepts was a key to getting results from MBM.

Still another problem, also caused by the deficiency in personal knowledge, was a tendency to apply MBM as a rigid formula—rather like a solution looking for a problem, instead of the other way around. Rigidly defining the particulars and prescribing exactly how MBM should be applied undermines its usefulness and adaptability. Learning how to recognize and resist this natural tendency (which is the hallmark of bureaucracies everywhere) has been another important step forward. "A foolish consistency is the hobgoblin of little minds, adored by little statesmen and philosophers and divines," wrote Emerson.[4]

We are now better at detecting and dealing with such tendencies, but we are still, and always will be, far from perfect. We try to enforce only general principles and themes, freeing people to challenge the particulars. Even so, "there is no such thing as instant pudding," to quote Deming.[5]

In order to fully capture the power of MBM, not only must an organization avoid unproductive tendencies; it should continually strive to improve its ability to internalize and apply beneficial mental models. This requires a willingness to undergo the most difficult and painful of all changes: a change in one's thinking.

Accomplishing such a change involves a focused and prolonged effort to develop new habits of thinking based on valid mental models. Developing these new habits involves a sustained transformation, akin to a bodybuilder retraining himself to run marathons. It's a long-term commitment. I should know; I've been working at it for more than fifty years.

Deep-seated habits are the result of neurological pathways in one's brain that are extremely difficult to eliminate and replace. That's why culture is so hard to change. And it's a big reason why businesses stagnate and their employees adopt a herd mentality: the natural tendency is to stick with familiar mental models and ways of doing things. To get results, brain rewiring is essential. This kind of change is the key to making the discoveries that lead to innovation and, in turn, good profit.

Here is how that process occurs. As we study a particular field, we absorb increasing amounts of specific knowledge, including rules, facts, terminology, and relationships. At some point, we know these details well enough that we can begin to focus on the whole.

Then we start to see patterns, the meaning of things, and sense when something is wrong—even though we may not always be able to articulate our understanding. This improves our ability to perceive problems and opportunities—whether when researching a new technology or market, interviewing a candidate, screening an acquisition, or doing anything with the goal of delivering value to both the customer and the company.

The process of discovery begins when we observe, often vaguely, a gap between what is and what could be. Our intuition tells us something better is just beyond the range of our mind's eye. To build a culture of discovery, we must encourage, not discourage, the passionate pursuit of hunches (no matter their origin).

Next, we need to strive—seeking help when needed—to clearly articulate our hypotheses, which, when made concrete and specific, can be challenged, tested, and improved to the point that we believe them to be valid. Hypotheses that pass this hurdle can then be put to the broader test of implementation.

The genesis of this entire process is the development of personal knowledge that is passionately applied to capture an opportunity or solve a problem.

To its credit, the MBM Development Group pioneered several useful improvements, such as the greatly expanded use of scorecards measuring how and where Koch creates value, how it stacks up to competitors on the use of resources and other measures, and whether and how it is improving.

All this helped us more fully appreciate the value of having measures based on economic reality. It reminded us that to guide activity correctly we must measure what leads to results, rather than what is easy to measure. This is why if an evaluation of an employee's performance includes only her contribution to current profits rather than her effect on long-term profits and culture, we inadvertently encourage work on the wrong things.

Although the Development Group no longer exists, its formation was an important early step in codifying MBM and educating all Koch employees, not just leaders. In its place we now have the MBM Capability, which has a different vision: to constantly develop new MBM tools and to teach and consult on the application of MBM. It has over forty members, many of whom have practical business experience and are proven result getters.

Around 1995, we developed a breakthrough called the MBM Toolkit, which addresses how to holistically apply the five dimensions in a way that captures their full power. We call this approach the Problem-Solving Process, and we've found that it greatly improves the ability of our employees to capture opportunities and to innovate. This will be further discussed in chapter 11.

This success fed on itself, because it demonstrated to everyone the power of the MBM framework. As a result, more people became willing to undertake what Polanyi called the "self-modifying act of conversion"[6] necessary to put a new way of thinking into practice. In our case, this involved applying all five dimensions of MBM to get results—whether in dealing with a customer, on the factory floor, or in the office.

Our rate of improvement at getting results from MBM has accelerated over the last decade. A key driver has been our recognition that all leaders, not just members of the MBM Capability, must own MBM and the culture in their groups. The role of the MBM Capability is to equip and support them.

This means that a key expectation of all our leaders is to understand and apply MBM themselves, and to drive that understanding and application throughout the organization, starting with their direct reports. When a leader at any level does not take these steps, performance and progress lag. For those leaders who do undertake the "self-modifying act of conversion" to understand and apply MBM, the improvement throughout their business is rapid and marked.

The following chapters will show what happens in an organization when people embrace a deep personal knowledge of MBM, and what happens when people underutilize or merely pay lip service to MBM.

CHAPTER 5

Learning from Adversity

KOCH'S MAJOR FAILURES IN APPLYING MBM

Adversity doth best discover virtue.
—FRANCIS BACON[1]

When I read this quote from Francis Bacon, a philosopher of science called the "father of empiricism," I am reminded of what my own father wrote in the letter he left his sons: "Adversity is a blessing in disguise and certainly is the greatest character builder."

In my mind, this wisdom was as valuable as the company he left us—especially when I recall what it took to get through the 1990s, the decade in which Koch's worst managerial and compliance failures made headlines. Indeed, despite its success, our company has endured several horrible events, some of which were the result of our own shortcomings.

Such disasters certainly create adversity for all who are hurt by them, but they can be "a blessing in disguise" for those who, as a result, are saved from future adversity. It's painful to me, for sure. I can never undo all the damage that has been done, but I can commit myself to improving as a result of these management failures and helping others avoid the same mistakes.

These experiences brought home for me the fact that if Koch

Industries becomes complacent, not only will creative destruction drive us out of business; serious harm to others may result. No wonder, then, that we strive to maintain a palpable sense of unease inside the company and guard against self-assuredness. None of us at Koch can ever declare victory and lose focus on what matters. This chapter is about the lessons we learned from these devastating failures and how those lessons informed and guided our subsequent refinement and improvement in the application of MBM.

In August 1996, something terrible happened. A leak from one of our gas liquids pipelines caused an explosion in Lively, Texas. I have seen reports of many industrial accidents over the years, including some fatalities. But that horrific incident in Lively was, to my knowledge, the first and only time since our company's founding in 1940 that one of our pipelines caused the death of innocent bystanders.

Two teenagers, Danielle Smalley and Jason Stone, smelled something suspicious near the pipeline and got in their car to alert authorities. When sparks from the car's ignition ignited the fumes from the leaking pipeline, they were killed in the resulting flames. Koch was at fault and readily admitted it. What happened was unacceptable and caused the death of two innocent teenagers and enormous pain to their families and community.

That was one of my darkest days on the job. I am a father and grandfather, and if anything like this were to happen to my own children or grandchildren, I know I would be devastated. I am also an engineer who places the highest priority on safety and compliance. In fact, I constantly insist it is "Job One" for every Koch employee. Why? Because I cherish the value of human life.

I am no stranger to suffering and death. My brother David, with whom I have shared a lifelong closeness, nearly died on a Los Angeles runway in 1991 when his US Air flight landed on another plane—an accident caused by an air-traffic controller's error. My brother barely escaped the burning cabin and spent the next two days in an intensive care unit. Twenty-three of his fellow passengers perished in the flames and toxic smoke.

In 1959, I helped extract a friend from his overturned automobile as he bled profusely. Minutes earlier he had been visiting my Boston home with his date. She survived the crash, but within half an hour my friend had died.

As the employer of many military veterans, I often hear their accounts of maiming and death—some from accidental causes, others from combat. I am horrified by the suffering they have witnessed and endured.

I have mentioned all of these events for a reason. Across the United States, there are thousands of industrial fatalities and a much greater number of serious on-the-job injuries each year. At Koch, we reject the notion that serious injury or the loss of life is an inevitable reality for employees of a large manufacturing company. This is why we have since improved our application of MBM to ensure that we always strive to go beyond standard industry practice on safety when appropriate, and only employ leaders and other employees who do so.

The tragedy in Lively taught us several important lessons that have improved our approach to safety. The pipeline in question was fifteen years old and had been closed in 1992 due to corrosion concerns. In 1995, it was reopened after we replaced all the corroded parts of the pipeline and then ran a hydrotest to demonstrate it was safe to operate.

The corrosion that led to the explosion was caused by bacteria in the soil that acted more quickly than leading U.S. experts had ever found. (In court, the plaintiff's expert witness had to look to Canada to find an example of such fast-acting and corrosive bacteria.) This rapid corrosion in Texas caught us off guard and caused the disaster.

In MBM terms, this was a knowledge failure. Realizing that, we applied the MBM principles to identify the source and cause of the problem and worked with the National Transportation and Safety Board to share this knowledge throughout the pipeline industry. Koch then used the knowledge learned from this incident to modify its operating procedures to help avoid any repeat of such a tragic accident. These improvements have not been simply inserted into the employee handbook or put on a page of the company website. They have been incorporated in MBM and transmitted throughout Koch. In addition, we have committed R&D resources to develop new anticorrosion measures, such as corrosion sensors in cooperation with Molex and the new nylon pipe from INVISTA mentioned in chapter 3.

Unfortunately, Koch faced another crisis (thankfully not fatal) around the same time in Corpus Christi, Texas. This crisis was caused by failures to apply fully both the Virtue and Talents and Decision Rights dimensions of MBM.

In the spring of 1995, an employee of Koch Petroleum Group (now called Flint Hills Resources) filed a false report about the Corpus Christi refinery's waste streams, as required by the newly expanded Clean Air Act. The employee (an environmental engineer who didn't make the measurements required, but invented numbers instead to plug into the report) stated that Corpus Christi was in compliance with the new regulations. We later determined this was not true.

When we found out what he had done, he was terminated, and Koch Petroleum Group voluntarily disclosed the incorrect filing to Texas's state environmental protection agency at a meeting we requested on November 27, 1995. At that meeting, we presented our findings and promised to report back on the details of the noncompliance as we uncovered more information. The ten MBM Guiding Principles (see chapter 7) are central to everything we do, and the first two are Integrity and Compliance. The report filed by a Koch employee was a clear violation of both these principles and could not be tolerated or allowed to reoccur.

At subsequent meetings, KPG provided the promised details of noncompliance, proposed a fine similar to what other companies had received, and discussed appropriate reporting methodology for the next report, due in April 1996.

But what appeared to be an issue that should have been resolved at the state level, with a civil remedy, ended up becoming a federal criminal case—one that introduced Koch to the many imperfections of the American criminal justice system. This experience influenced in part our decision to consider the job applications of people with prior felony convictions, rather than ruling them out at the start.

More than four years after making the disclosure to the state, Koch, KPG, and four employees were prosecuted by the U.S. Department of Justice in Washington for alleged violations of federal environmental law and false statements.

What made this a criminal case, rather than a civil one, was a mistaken belief that Koch had covered up aspects of the violation when it made its disclosure to the Texas agency. We were confident that a grand jury would understand this wasn't true. We had, after all, fully disclosed our violation to the state regulators back in 1995.

To us, knowing KPG had voluntarily self-disclosed this issue, the claim that our people had tried to deceive the regulators seemed suspicious from the start. And though we didn't learn about this until long after the indictments were issued and the case was headed for trial, our suspicions were confirmed by a stunning development: The DOJ lawyers presented the grand jury with a Texas state document that had been altered in a way that caused Koch to appear guilty of a cover-up.

The original document summarizing KPG's November 1995 discussion with state regulators concluded with the information that KPG had self-disclosed it was out of compliance. "They will investigate further and return with a follow-up in early February with the [sic] how far and how long they have been out of compliance."

But the grand jury was presented with another version of that document, retyped almost word for word—except for the inexplicable omission of the words "how far and how long they have been out of compliance." In other words, the grand jury had indicted the company and four innocent employees based on what appears to be intentional fraud.

Experiencing firsthand what the criminal justice system can do to a company—and worse, to its individual employees—has made me more skeptical of the criminal justice system and some criminal convictions. But it also reinforced our already strong commitment to never become complacent about compliance.

The Department of Justice's ninety-seven-count indictment was eventually reduced to seven counts. Outside experts advised KPG to plead guilty to a criminal charge, pay a fine, and move on. These experts also advised that the company should leave the indicted employees to fend for themselves against the government and turn over all attorney-client information to the government, which could then be used against the employees.

We refused to do so because we did not believe the four indicted employees had done anything wrong. For us to treat our people in this manner would be a violation of our Guiding Principles. The case proceeded toward trial with the government unsuccessfully pressuring our employees to falsely implicate more senior Koch officials in return for leniency. The prosecution even called as a witness the terminated employee who had filed the false report.

The prosecution also relied heavily on the testimony of another former KPG employee, who was an environmental engineer. Before quitting, she had been informed her job performance was unacceptable and warned she would be terminated if she didn't improve. Now acting as a "whistle-blower," she told the state that our subsequent environmental report was also false. This employee testified that she was concerned about getting fired months before blowing the whistle, and had consulted with multiple plaintiff's attorneys about suing KPG (which she did, and we settled).

She also told a coworker that when she went to the state, she had a plan to force the company to fire her. When that plan failed, she resigned but misrepresented that fact to the state in order to receive unemployment benefits.

Here again there were lessons to be learned. First and foremost, KPG had failed to follow our MBM Virtue and Talents dimension by not terminating this employee for her performance failures after she resisted efforts to help her improve. Instead of making tough decisions, her supervisors had transferred her around the refinery, trying to work with her to improve her performance.

In addition, the way the Corpus Christi refinery handled the noncompliance issue with the new regulations was inconsistent with MBM's Decision Rights dimension. Individuals responsible for day-to-day issues tried to investigate the noncompliance and then deal with the government regulator. This was also a mistake. Today, Koch would request different individuals to investigate noncompliance—people who were not involved with the underlying issues or the day-to-day refinery operations.

Filing a false report with the government can be a felony, so it's essential to bring in company employees with better knowledge—or even better, outside experts to investigate and answer to regulators.

The government's case ultimately collapsed a few weeks before trial in a hearing before a federal judge, after Koch finally had an opportunity to challenge the government's key expert witness: an Environmental Protection Agency investigator who admitted the wastewater samples collected by the "whistle-blower" and used as evidence of KPG's noncompliance were unreliable, as their collection was not consistent with EPA requirements for sampling. Other than the information Koch supplied as part of its voluntary self-disclosure to the Texas environmental agency, the DOJ did not provide any other support for its allegations. And so all of the charges against Koch and the four indicted employees were dismissed.

In April 2001, KPG pled guilty to one new single count—the false report made by the former employee it had disclosed in November 1995. The government made the four innocent employees sign an agreement promising not to sue for malicious prosecution, as a condition of dropping the charges against them. Though they were ultimately exonerated, what happened to these four employees was beyond the pale.

So how did we use the lessons from this unfortunate incident to better apply MBM across all our companies? To start with, we took additional steps to ensure that all our businesses were fully implementing our Virtue and Talents dimension. As you'll read more about in chapter 7, we increased our efforts to hire first on values, and only then on talent and experience. Today, if we find existing employees have questionable integrity or lack commitment to safety or compliance, we terminate them.

This is an obligation of every leader at every level. If a leader doesn't fully perform this difficult role, he does not belong in a position with supervisory responsibilities. Had our Corpus Christi facility been operating in this manner, there would have been no issues. Following this incident, we had to face the reality that we needed to improve our internal and external practices.

There are tens of thousands of laws and regulations that apply to our businesses, many with the potential to impose criminal liability on the company and its employees. Based on this reality, and these incidents in the mid-1990s, we developed our 10,000 percent compliance model, which reminds employees that 100 percent compliance is required 100 percent of the time. It is designed to avoid incidents like these from ever occurring, by helping employees remember to "stop, think, and ask" whenever an issue arises about which they are not 100 percent certain.

While we can never declare victory, I am relieved that Koch has not faced any further indictments or prosecutions for more than a decade. Making the 10,000 percent model a reality requires holding everyone in the management chain responsible for performance—even when he doesn't know a problem exists.

These incidents also prompted us to look at how we dealt with regulators and whether we treated them with the appropriate level

of respect and customer focus. We deal with a great many regulators on a daily basis at our facilities. We realized that we needed
to better understand and satisfy their needs just like we would a
commercial customer. Our mental models needed to take into account the reality that without government approval, business can't
operate in this country.

I am proud to say that since these incidents, the EPA has recognized Koch's companies' environmental performance and steward-
ship many times, commenting on the productive and collaborative
approach that Koch companies use in working with the agency.
For example, the emissions from our refineries are 31 percent
lower than our refinery peer group on a per barrel process basis.[2]
In its Toxic Release Inventory report published in 2015, the EPA
ranked Koch the best U.S.-based parent company for implementing pollution prevention initiatives.[3] We have MBM to thank for
these improvements.

Koch has applied the lessons learned from these past legal problems to our current businesses, and to the due diligence we employ
when evaluating potential acquisitions. These incidents reinforce
the great emphasis MBM places on culture and on hiring people
based not just on skills but on virtues, with the goal of ensuring
our businesses and leaders foster integrity, courage, compliance,
and respect. This is why Koch's senior leaders travel around the
world for town hall meetings with their employees to discuss the
importance of a compliance culture.

In part because of these incidents, wherever and whenever we
find a problem, we immediately apply the MBM framework to
remedy the issue, especially if it involves safety, the environment,
or compliance. This includes shutting an operation down or even
divesting it, if we don't believe it can be made to meet our standards.

Because there is no stronger form of communication than face-
to-face sharing, we also now ask employees who lived through the
Corpus Christi and Lively incidents to meet with new employees

who weren't with the company at the time. The senior leaders explain to the employees the pain and stress these incidents caused for all involved, including their families.

The goal is not only to educate employees on the facts of these cases, but to convey their heavy emotional toll. This process is key to reaching the hearts and minds of our employees and helping them understand why we put such an emphasis on 10,000 percent compliance. We use the same approach in the aftermath of accidents, no matter how minor, in order to ensure that people internalize the human cost of these incidents firsthand.

I cannot fully address the issue of adversity without mentioning a third case involving Koch that made headlines throughout the 1990s. I don't believe it was driven by either a Virtue and Talents or a Decision Rights failure, but rather by a shareholder dispute.

In 1989, Koch was sued in a False Claims Act case in an Oklahoma federal court. This case was filed by David's twin, my brother Bill, a former shareholder who had sued the company repeatedly and unsuccessfully throughout the 1980s. The case revolved around Koch's oil measurement practices on federal and Indian lands from 1975 through 1988.

During that time, Koch Oil had become the largest crude oil gatherer in the country because of its superior customer service. Given the field conditions and imprecise hand gauging used to measure oil at that time, we believe that our practices were, at the very least, consistent with—and in many respects better than—industry practice. In fact, the evidence showed that Koch's gauging practices were close to 99.5 percent accurate, which was above the industry standard. Considering that Koch focused on servicing independent producers, many of whom were located in remote areas with challenging field conditions, such accuracy is even more impressive. Incrustation, gas in the oil, BS&W (the acronym for the basic sediment and water in the bottom of an oil tank), temperature variation across the tank, misshapen tanks, and a host of other variables come into play, making 100 percent accuracy unattainable.

Because Koch's recorded oil sales exceeded its recorded oil purchases, the lawsuit claimed we improperly took the oil and went so
far as to claim Koch had "stolen" the oil.

None of our customers sued us or joined in this litigation, nor
did any testify against Koch in the case. In fact, some customers
testified for us at the trial, saying if they ever had concerns with
Koch's measurements, they raised questions and any issues were
resolved amicably by mutual agreement.

Even the Osage Indian tribe voiced support for Koch throughout the case, and the Federal Bureau of Land Management found
no wrongdoing on our part, reporting "no discrepancies or irregu-
larities in production accountability" had been shown.[4]

Unfortunately, some disgruntled former employees—the vast
majority of whom were terminated for theft or other violations of
company policy—testified against Koch. These former employees
offered vague allegations that they had "stolen" oil, but had never
made such a claim prior to the lawsuit. In fact, no oil was "stolen,"
and there was no finding of theft in this case.

Yet the U.S. District Court for the Northern District of Oklahoma instructed the jury that Koch's customers could not bind the
government, and it was irrelevant whether our customers approved
of the measurements at the time they were made. Because of the
special rules that govern oil leases controlled by the federal government, all that mattered, according to the court, was whether the
amount of oil submitted on a claim form was different from what
actually was paid for. After more than a week of deliberations, the
jury returned a verdict against Koch. The case settled in 2001.

Applying MBM to this case in retrospect, I believe it started
with a conflict of vision among Koch Industries' shareholders. Disagreement stemming from that conflict led to mistrust, then de-
generated into lawsuits, a 1983 buyout, and years of even more
lawsuits.

The lack of an effective vision, or, as in this case, a conflict of
vision, is a root cause of the failure of many great businesses. This
is why today, with every single hire Koch makes, we are seeking

honorable people who share a vision for a better world—a world where business succeeds by making people better off.

The next chapter explains the first of MBM's five dimensions—the one that is absolutely essential to get right at the outset, before addressing the other four. It is vision.

PART II

CHAPTER 6

Vision

GUIDE TO AN UNKNOWN FUTURE

Whatever you can do, or dream you can, begin it. Bold-
ness has genius, magic, and power in it!

—GOETHE (ATTRIBUTED)[1]

I was well past my seventieth birthday when I first saw the words
"Koch brothers" paired together in the media. Although there
are four of us, most people who use the phrase are only refer-
ring to David and me, the two who remained with the company
after Frederick and Bill sold their shares in 1983.

David lives in Manhattan with his wife and three children,
where he is a high-profile patron of the arts and benefactor of the
leading hospitals and cancer research centers in New York and the
United States. No wonder, then, that Barbara Walters included
David on her television special *The 10 Most Fascinating People of
2014*.

David's selection highlights the difference in our lifestyles. His
is interesting; mine is not. When I am not at the office, I'm either
studying praxeology, working out in our basement gym, analyzing the twenty-four components of the golf swing, enjoying one of
Liz's "heart-healthy" meals in our kitchen, or trying to understand

what my toddler grandsons are saying when we FaceTime. (Charlie, the older one, calls me Poppy—which is much kinder than what the media sometimes call me. He picked that up from Liz, who called me Poppy even before I became a grandparent.)

Despite our superficial differences—as well as our very fundamental ones (David likes ballet; I like football)—David and I have gotten along as business partners for half a century because we have always shared the same vision for Koch: to innovate, grow, and reinvest in order to maximize long-term value by applying our core capabilities.

A VISION SHARED BY PARTNERS

Short-term profits, while necessary, are not sufficient for long-term business success. Each business must take to heart what Schumpeter called capitalism's essential role: driving "the perennial gale of creative destruction."[2] To succeed in the long term, a business must innovate and improve at least as fast as its most effective competitor. David and I understand that creative destruction must be integral to Koch Industries' vision. This is an essential difference that sets us apart from many other companies.

Our commitment to long-term profitability is fortified by our partners, the Marshall family, who are significant shareholders. J. Howard Marshall II, his son Pierce, and Pierce's widow, Elaine, have been resolute allies of ours even when our vision came under fire.

The Marshalls have always joined David and me in our vision of aiming to maintain a growth rate of roughly 12 percent or higher. When compounded, that growth rate enables us to double our earnings, on average, every six years. The "on average" modifier is critically important, because if we try to smooth out earnings (as some public companies feel compelled to do to defend their stock price) our future would not be as bright. Koch's emphasis on compounding (sometimes called "the most powerful force in the universe") is another difference between the vision of our company and that of many others.

Doubling our earnings in six years requires that we continually improve our ability to more fully and broadly apply MBM; that we add and develop the talent to function effectively as a much larger, more complex company; that we remain private so we can focus on the long term; that we generate the opportunities to enable us to reinvest 90 percent of our earnings at superior returns; and that we ensure that all employees, everywhere, behave with integrity and compliance. (These two principles are at the top of our list of MBM Guiding Principles, which will be described in the next chapter.)

For any company to increase good profit at this rate, the right vision—combined with the right values—is essential. This starts with having the right partners, those who share vision and values. When partners don't have shared vision and values, dissolution of that marriage may become necessary. My advice is to get a "business prenup."

To be locked into a hostile partnership with no separation mechanism is a nightmare. At best, it becomes a stalemate in which nothing can be decided, and the business atrophies. We had one joint venture in which the hostile partner started showing up an hour and a half late for board meetings only to veto everything. Fortunately, our agreement included a divorce procedure and we were able to attain separation. We learned some time ago to avoid entering into partnerships without an exit mechanism.

When the parties do share vision and values, and contribute according to their comparative advantages, the partnership can be a powerful vehicle for superior value creation. Our purchase of Chrysler Realty mentioned in chapter 3 was made possible because of the partnership we formed with Wichita entrepreneur George Ablah. Thanks to our shared vision of buying and upgrading distressed properties, and the values we had in common, that partnership was very successful.

Creating an effective vision is the first dimension of MBM, and the genesis of the good profit that leads to long-term success. That's because until you envision what your business should be, and how it will create value for others, there is no way to know which talents, knowledge processes, decision rights, and incentives will be necessary. (The virtues required for good profit remain constant, no matter what the vision.) Vision is foundational for the other four dimensions.

SETTING YOUR SIGHTS

There are those who see profit as a necessary evil at best—a sign of greed, and something that comes about through "exploitation" or hoodwinking the consumer. For them, all profit is bad.

Thomas Sowell eloquently counters this assumption when he writes, "To the economically illiterate, if some company makes a million dollars in profit, this means that their products cost a million dollars more than they would have without profits. It never occurs to such people that these products might cost several million dollars more . . . without the incentives to be efficient created by the prospect of profits."[3]

It's safe to say that few of those who hold this view have ever experienced what it actually means to earn a profit over the long term by making others' lives better. If they had, they would appreciate, as I do, good profit. They'd see that in a truly free society, people and businesses gain by serving others.

"Consumption is the sole end and purpose of production; and the interest of the producer ought to be attended to only so far as it may be necessary for promoting that of the consumer,"[4] wrote Adam Smith.

Consumption drives Koch's vision. I say that in the same spirit Smith did, with respect for the consumer on the other side of the equation guiding my actions. Whether she is "consuming" fuels, food, paper products, books, biotechnology, or information technology, my purpose in business is to serve that person.

If producers knew not only what consumers want now, but what they will want in the future, their job would be pretty easy. In fact, if *consumers* knew what consumers wanted now and in the future, a producer's job would be pretty easy.

But no one knows. Sometimes consumers aren't even aware they need a new product or service, or have a frustration with an old one, until the new one is introduced to them. Having a business vision for this open-ended evolution of consumer want is critical to long-term success.

When large information technology users in the 1970s were asked what computers they would use in the future, 70 percent said IBM mainframes. They never envisioned the idea of $500 personal computers networked to form the Internet, let alone smartphones and tablets. Over-reliant on its vision of mainframe dominance, IBM was slow getting into the personal computer business, and even then did not succeed.

"The solution of the economic problem is a voyage of exploration into the unknown, an attempt to discover new ways of doing things better. Economic problems are created by unforeseen changes which require adaptation,"[5] wrote Hayek.

Hayek understood that the future is unknown and unknowable, so we can never predict with certainty which investments will be profitable. To drive creative destruction internally, we must develop numerous well founded experiments to determine which new products, processes, methods, organizational forms, and businesses will be successful.

In deciding which businesses to pursue, Koch looks at how we can make good profit in the long term. This is fundamental to our vision because unless a business creates value for others, it will cease to exist (unless coercion is involved).

History has shown that continually profitable organizations are those that provide what people value. Businesses that don't, like the ninety-three companies that have disappeared from the original Forbes 100 list since 1917, tend to die out.

I suspect a flawed vision was partly to blame for the demise of those companies. They failed to understand how to continue to create superior value in society over the long term. As a result, they did less and less of that as time went on. For any business to sustain success, Koch included, we must have a vision that guides us to do more and more for our customers and society.

PEOPLE, NOT THINGS

Koch's Vision is different from most because it's focused on value creation and people. You'll notice in our statement opposite that we don't even mention a product or industry. Instead, we focus on what we can do for *people* by fulfilling the role of business in people's lives. Koch's Vision addresses the specific capabilities our people need to develop and apply, and the benefits we deliver to people in society when we do so.

In a truly free economy, for a business to survive and prosper in the long term it must develop and use its capabilities to create real, sustainable, superior value for its customers, for society, and for itself. Only by doing so can it continue to inspire and attract customers, suppliers, and partners.

When any of these parties has a choice of whom to work with, we want it to be Koch. If Koch isn't their counterparty of choice, we're not offering them more value than our competitors and won't be as successful as we can be.

Having a clear vision is critical to attracting the best talent, as well. Understanding what a business is trying to achieve and how it creates value—in other words, its vision—not only enables employees to focus and prioritize; it helps them develop and find fulfillment. Having a shared vision guides the development of roles, responsibilities, and expectations. That's why getting the vision right, helping employees (especially leaders) internalize it, and updating it as often as necessary is essential.

Koch's Vision was updated in 2013 to more accurately reflect our practice and what is needed to continue our success in the future:

> The role of business in society is to help people improve their lives by providing products and services they value more highly than their alternatives, and to do so while consuming fewer resources. To the extent a business does this by the economic means, its profits are a measure of the value it creates in society. Creative destruction is inherent in a market system, so a business must not only continually improve the value it creates for customers and society, but do so significantly faster than its competitors.
>
> Thus, to continue to succeed, our Vision is to improve the value we create for our customers more efficiently and faster than our competitors. This should enable us to generate the return on capital and investment opportunities needed to achieve a long-term growth rate that doubles earnings, on average, every six years. This necessitates significantly accelerating the application of MBM, becoming much more forward-looking in talent acquisition and development, remaining private and continuing to reinvest 90 percent of earnings, while conducting all affairs lawfully and with integrity.

To achieve these goals we must improve our return on capital and substantially increase the origination and capture of investment opportunities. Our investment focus will be on those opportunities that—by utilizing existing or adding new capabilities—provide the greatest value creation, the highest returns and contribution, and new growth platforms.

This is Koch's Vision. But every company, no matter what size or type, should strive to develop and clearly communicate a unique vision of its own.

FROM PAPER TOWELS TO THE INTERNET OF THINGS

Several steps are necessary when developing a vision. The first is creating a view of how the organization can create superior value for its customers and society and capture a share of it. The vision is a description of exactly how the organization plans to create that value.

Some of the capabilities that are critical to Koch's ability to create superior value are commercial excellence, operations excellence, talent, innovation, a trading mentality, and public sector effectiveness. MBM is the overarching capability that is vital to achieving Koch's vision. Other businesses have different capabilities, and understanding what those are and how they can create superior value are key to developing an effective vision.

Any organization interested in good profit should begin with a realistic assessment of what it can do particularly well that enables it to outperform others. Then it should address how to improve those capabilities and acquire the new ones needed to keep pace in the future. This includes working or partnering with other organizations that have superior complementary capabilities, such as the twenty organizations with which INVISTA has alliances to accelerate progress in developing biochemical processes.

Finally, the vision should serve as a guide to other opportunities for which any combination of these capabilities can create superior value.

Central to this capabilities-focused vision is Principled Entrepreneurship, which must embrace the spirit of creative destruction. To maximize growth in the long term, business needs to commit to a high reinvestment rate that recognizes the power of compounding. Taken together, these factors are what sets Koch's vision apart from many other companies. These were the elements that led Sterling Varner and me away from the vision of gathering crude oil in southern Oklahoma to becoming the leader in gathering crude in North America. These elements have been the basis for the visions of our businesses ever since.

Considering all the new capabilities Koch has acquired and developed over the years, it's impossible to predict all the ways in which we will apply our philosophy in the future. Because the future is unknown and unknowable, a company's vision needs to be open-ended and to embrace creative destruction on a fundamental level.

In our experience, a company tends to be better served when it is capability-focused rather than industry-focused. In the oil industry, for example, there is no reason why a successful exploration company must also be in refining and marketing. Even though all these are facets of the same industry, the capabilities required for oil exploration are quite different from those required for other parts of the value chain. A company doesn't need to own or control its feedstock supply when, like crude oil, it is widely available on liquid markets. A company only needs to do so when supply is not liquid, or when having control in a particular location gives the company a cost or quality advantage.

For this reason, although oil refining is an important business for us, we have not felt the need to have our own crude oil production to supply our refineries, or our own service stations to provide an outlet for our products. Instead, we have built trading, distribution, and transportation capabilities.

We're involved in a modest amount of oil exploration only because we have been able to make it a successful stand-alone business by applying our trading mentality, which involves continually modifying our investment strategies as the relative markets for acreage and reserves change (see appendix C).

An example of the unpredictability of our future directions—and the role of vision in guiding them—is our acquisition of Georgia-Pacific, which set in motion an evolutionary path that started with paper towels and led to exploration of how limitless and low-cost connectivity between objects, machines, and people (the Internet of Things) can create value in both manufacturing plants and offices.

It's not too hard to envision a "washroom of the future," with sensors monitoring peak usage times, hygiene patterns, and mold potential while automatically reordering bathroom tissue, towels, and soap. This technology could improve sanitation, reduce costs, and streamline communications between GP and commercial building owners.

How did we get from paper towels to such an idea? When Koch acquired Georgia-Pacific in 2005, its enMotion® hands-free paper towel dispenser had been helping people avoid germs in public restrooms since 2002. GP has managed to sustain its core paper products business while impressively growing market share for en-Motion products.

But in the spirit of creative destruction, the new Koch vision for GP encouraged multiple types and generations of experimental discovery in the world of paper-dispensing products. Innovations included new cabinet designs, quieter versions with smaller footprints, improved towel features, extension into soap dispensing, and free performance upgrades and replacements for existing enMotion installations. The introduction of SofPull® towel dispensers provided a lower-priced alternative. Between 2005 and 2009, paper sales from the original enMotion business doubled.

But then, in 2009, GP's sales plateaued as Schumpeter's "perennial gale" blew through. Remaining competitive requires more than just product innovations. It also requires new technologies, new sources of supply, and new types of organization.

So we began to consider how sensors—not just paper towels—could help people improve their lives. People valued not having to touch a dispenser's handle with wet hands in a public restroom, where germs abound. How else could sensor technology provide customers with value?

By keeping its focus on *people*, GP has begun exciting work on the wireless monitoring of dispenser use, so that hospitals can help improve the hand hygiene habits of health-care providers. By reminding hospital personnel to wash their hands before they touch someone, this technology can play a critical role in reducing the rate of patient infections.

Although growth in paper sales from the original enMotion dispenser has slowed since 2009, additional innovations have enabled sales for the entire business to grow more than ten times faster than the market. Electronic touchless systems now have more than a 15 percent share of the away-from-home hand-drying market, with GP owning well over half of that.

The Internet of Things is also of obvious interest to Molex, Koch's second-largest acquisition. An innovative electronics manufacturer, Molex is exploring "digital ceilings" in commercial buildings. These incorporate LED lighting with integrated sensor arrays, networked using standard Cat5 Ethernet cable, which reduces installation costs for consumers, conserves energy by optimizing voltage according to detected usage, and can be customized to satisfy the local needs of employees.

Molex is leading an initiative to develop new sensors and find innovative applications across Koch. In 2015, Molex began working with Flint Hills Resources' Corpus Christi refinery and INVISTA's Victoria, Texas, plant to explore new opportunities for using sensors to improve manufacturing processes.

At both companies, new sensor technology is being developed to enhance safety and conservation by detecting potential pipe and vessel leaks before they cause a problem. Sensors are also under development to monitor vibrations and anticipate malfunctions, prevent steam trap failure, detect hazardous gases in process areas, and help control process variables—all contributing not only to reliability, but to safer workplaces and communities.

By combining new sensor technology with Molex's other electronic capabilities, Koch has an opportunity to enhance safety, reduce costs, and create value for others. This is due in large part to our following a vision that focuses on what our employees can do to seize the opportunities to create value for our customers.

OPTIMIZING RESOURCES

"Run it hard—let it break—fix it." You probably wouldn't operate your car this way, but in the mid-1990s, Flint Hills' operating mentality focused on maximizing daily production instead of maximizing long-term value. Operators ran the equipment hard, around the clock, and when something finally broke, the operators would shut units down until a mechanic was available to make repairs.

Operators and mechanics were largely rewarded for maximizing short-term profitability, which meant long-term factors were underappreciated. But long-term thinking is a critical aspect of Principled Entrepreneurship—the most fundamental and distinguishing component of Koch's vision.

To achieve that vision of creating value for others while conserving resources, employees must think long-term like principled owners. Conservation is foundational to Principled Entrepreneurship. We aren't creating value in society if the resources we are consuming are worth more in another use than the value of the products we are making from them. We are also destroying value when we waste resources by not using them in the most efficient way.

If Principled Entrepreneurship were a coin, one side would be value creation for the customer. The other side would be conservation of resources—capital, raw materials, energy, labor, specialized skills, intellectual property, and time—so they are available to satisfy other needs in society. Maximizing that differential between value creation for the customer and consumption of resources is what we try to accomplish by practicing Principled Entrepreneurship.

In the late 1990s, finances and safety were both suffering at Flint Hills Resources. The leadership at FHR responded by developing a deeper appreciation of what it means to practice Principled Entrepreneurship. This required changing to a system in which both operations and maintenance were united with a shared vision: to deliver safe, predictable operations with high reliability and proactive, efficient maintenance.

The new vision, called ownership-based work systems, included the aspiration to be "operator of choice," meaning that if a community were going to allow only one process plant, it would choose ours.

The difference in outcomes brought about by this change in vision at FHR was dramatic. The Pine Bend refinery reduced losses from unplanned events by more than 50 percent. Both Pine Bend and the Corpus Christi refinery became industry benchmarks for Environment, Health, & Safety performance, reliability, and financial results. Other Koch companies have worked with the Operations Excellence Capability to apply this same model and have achieved similar improvements.

Energy conservation is another area in which Koch has made significant progress in recent years. Until 2009, when the Koch Energy Team was formed, this important resource was treated as just "a cost of doing business" and was ranked behind other operating costs such as maintenance and personnel.

After studying energy-related benchmarks and best practices, the energy team discovered that certain non-Koch companies had achieved greater progress in those areas. Those studies and the commitment in our vision to consuming fewer resources enabled the team to leverage internal and external knowledge to develop an energy improvement model and a set of best practices.

The model included measurement tools, an integrated site-by-site roll-up of energy savings projects and ideas, an annual energy best practice assessment to gauge progress, and energy conferences to promote knowledge sharing. When employees at a GP cellulose plant in Brunswick, Georgia, tracked their boiler's fuel oil usage with a daily scorecard, they saw an opportunity to cut costs and save energy at the same time by running the boiler in a different way. Knowledge sharing between the utilities department, the boiler's manufacturer, and GP's risk management group resulted in a 70 percent reduction in fuel oil consumed, and savings of $1.6 million a year.

During the last four years, we have identified and captured over $200 million in annual energy savings. Across Koch Industries, our businesses have made a number of important resource-conserving innovations, all while providing a superior level of safety and environmental performance, obtaining permits under increasingly burdensome requirements, and developing new construction techniques to soften shortages in skilled labor. Specific examples of these vision-driven improvements can be found in every Koch company.

For one, Koch Ag and Energy Solutions develops new products that increase crop yields by considerably improving crop nutrient utilization. It is estimated that up to 40 percent of all the nitrogen fertilizer that is applied in the field is not utilized by the plant. But with innovations such as AGROTAIN®, the amount lost is reduced to less than 10 percent. Koch Ag is increasing crop production, reducing the effect of fertilizers on the environment, and conserving costly resources.

Koch-Glitsch, a subsidiary that builds tower internal assemblies, now uses safer and much more efficient robotic welding technology. Flint Hills Resources has developed innovative ways to transport, process, and trade the large new supplies of North American crude oil. Koch's Human Resources has developed more effective methods for worldwide talent recruitment and payroll, benefiting from Molex's superior global capabilities in this area. These improvements demonstrate Koch's vision of consuming fewer resources across all our businesses.

Capital is also a critical resource that we strive to conserve and optimize, consistent with our vision, by allocating it to its highest and best use. This applies to our liquid assets as well as our businesses.

Prior to the current artificially low interest rate environment, our philosophy was to invest excess liquidity in short-term low-risk instruments. In order to get an attractive return on our growing liquidity in this new environment, our business development, treasury, and pension management groups created the capabilities to make more complex, higher-return investments.

These include making passive minority investments in companies such as American Greetings, and doing middle-market lending. We have been successful in these new strategies because we listen to our counterparties' particular needs and then design structures that suit both parties well. Especially in today's environment, when Koch can invest its liquidity profitably and our counterparty can obtain needed financing on terms that are favorable compared to its alternatives, it is a win-win situation. We strive to offer speed, certainty, confidentiality, efficient and responsive deal screening, and to concede terms that are important to the seller but not as important to us.

Capital optimization also requires the proper selection of businesses and assets in the portfolio, and recognizing whether and when to sell them. In general, an asset should be sold when a buyer will pay more than the owner's estimate of its remaining value. This can be when an industry's rate of change overcomes an owner's ability to innovate.

For example, the rapid increase in polyester plants being built in China resulted in dramatic innovations that reduced the construction costs of the newer plants and improved their operating efficiency. So in 2010, INVISTA sold its polyester plants to Indorama Ventures, since they fit that company's large-scale global polyester industry consolidation and innovation strategy.

In contrast, INVISTA Performance Technologies, the industry's leading polyester licensing business, benefited from that same growth and innovation in China, which helped IPT extend its licensing business into global spandex and nylon technologies.

At Koch Industries, we rarely sell assets that provide a core capability or platform for growth. As crude oil production in South Texas declined through the 1990s, we considered selling our Corpus Christi crude oil gathering systems. We are fortunate we kept the major ones, because they later put us in a much better position to handle the large amounts of crude oil production that emerged from Eagle Ford.

Naturally, every business wants to capture the most value for something it sells. To do so, it needs to consider the various reasons why an asset or business would be worth more to someone else. Potential purchasers might not believe the business will deteriorate as rapidly as the seller does. They might see synergies with a complementary business they own. Or they may have relevant capabilities or innovations the seller does not have. In short, a buyer almost always has a different vision.

POINT OF VIEW

For a vision to be effective, it must be based on the best knowledge an organization can develop. At Koch, this starts with the best understanding of our existing and potential capabilities. It includes the best knowledge of customers and what they value, the best knowledge of competitors and their strategies, and the best knowledge of any changes affecting the industry. To garner all this, leaders must solicit the best knowledge internally and externally and create a culture in which the best knowledge is used regardless of the source.

Before making an acquisition as large as Georgia-Pacific, we satisfied this requirement through our experience with GP's pulp business, INVISTA's branded consumer products businesses, and the knowledge gained from our efforts to acquire other forest and consumer products companies. In fact, we were able to acquire all of GP at an acceptable price only because we had done our research and learned it was in leadership transition and credit was tight after the dot-com crash. Actually, Koch was the only bidder.

A vital part of selecting the most attractive opportunities involves developing a point of view regarding realistic scenarios in industries of interest. Since the future is unknown and unknowable, this is not an undertaking that can be done with any certainty. After all, if businesses could use a formula to determine the future, the value of entrepreneurial activity would be eliminated.

But, although the future is unknowable, it is not unimaginable. As Ludwig von Mises put it: "The entrepreneurial idea that carries on and brings profit is precisely that idea which did not occur to the majority. It is not correct foresight as such that yields profits, but foresight better than that of the rest. The prize goes only to the dissenters, who do not let themselves be misled by the errors accepted by the multitude."[6]

Of course, superior foresight by itself does not win the prize. The entrepreneur must have the conviction, courage, and capabilities to *act on* that insight. This is what we did when we invested billions to improve and expand our refineries when others did not, or acquired Farmland's fertilizer business out of bankruptcy during a depressed period for the industry.

Having a better point of view than our competitors has been a key driver of our success, but we have a great deal of room for improvement. There are numerous examples where, if we had developed a somewhat better point of view, we could have avoided substantial losses or enjoyed much greater profits.

One example is the precipitous drop in polyester technical fiber prices mentioned earlier in this chapter. Another is the depth and duration of the collapse of the 2008 housing bubble that resulted from the combination of the Federal Reserve's monetary policies and distortions caused by Fannie Mae and Freddie Mac and lending regulations. We could have enjoyed even better profits by anticipating the sharp drop in natural gas prices in 2008. Had we seen that coming, our fertilizer and chemical businesses would have expanded even more than they did.

Given the diversity of businesses within Koch Industries, its Vision must, of necessity, be broad. In some companies with capabilities more specific than Koch's—mostly smaller ones—the vision needs to be more specific (as it is for Koch's individual businesses). The breadth of a company's vision should vary with the breadth of its capabilities.

At the same time, a business must have a vision specific enough to guide its strategies, decision making, allocation of resources, and the roles, responsibilities, and expectations of all employees. Each vision also needs to be aspirational in order to expand the thinking of leaders and employees throughout the organization.

Creating an effective vision requires developing a directionally correct point of view. This cannot be done without intensive, systematic, global study. This is why we study not only the history of a business or industry, but also existing and potential technologies, competitors, customers, applicable laws, and industry structure, and how all these factors are changing—both for industries in which we participate and for those we are considering.

We then analyze their value chains and cost structures, future demand for their products, competitive positions of participants, and other meaningful factors and trends. We seek to understand the future drivers and level of profitability for the various segments of relevant industries. Even so, we recognize that uncertainty guarantees that any point of view can, at best, only be directionally correct. We performed all these studies before acquiring Georgia-Pacific and Molex, and before INVISTA moved forward with a major nylon complex in Shanghai.

Based on our changing point of view, we modify our thinking about the best opportunities and how to capture them. From this analysis, each business develops a vision that explicitly states how it plans to create superior value. These visions must be based on and consistent with Koch's Vision.

Achieving our goal of doubling earnings, on average, every six years necessitates continued improvement of our return on capital and an increased ability to generate and capture sufficiently profitable investment opportunities. The latter requires that our horizons increase with our size. We need innovations that move the needle, investments that make a bigger contribution, and new platforms that deliver growth.

All organizations can do this by developing a vision based on understanding their capabilities, and being committed to rapidly improving their ability to create value for their customers. This requires a culture of creative destruction. Molex, for example, has products with a life span as short as two to three years.

Disruptive innovation is a company's lifeblood to which significant human and financial resources must be dedicated. Intel cofounder Gordon Moore correctly determined that the performance of semi-conductors would double about every eighteen months. This is creative destruction at its most terrifying extreme and it is responsible for the 90 percent failure rate of technology start-ups. Now, more than ever, if you don't have a culture of innovation, your days are numbered.

BUSINESS IS RISKY

The vision development process applies equally to industries a company is in and those it is considering entering. New opportunities exist in a company's traditional industries just as they do in new ones. This is why Koch companies can apply the same vision development process inside or outside their current industries.

A starting point in this process is taking into account the capabilities of both the business and Koch Industries as a whole. The more difficult part is getting our businesses to focus on opportunities with enough potential to make a difference to Koch, given its size.

Based on its vision, Koch (and each of its businesses) develops and implements strategies that will maximize long-term value. We can only do so if we set priorities. In any complex business, deciding the order in which to do things can be just as important as deciding what things to do.

At least two sets of criteria are needed to determine priorities. The first set includes those actions that are required to simply stay in business, such as meeting a deadline for complying with a government regulation or a customer's quality requirements.

The second set is determined by comparing an estimate of the risk-adjusted present value of opportunities to the resources consumed. This means looking at not only the return on capital, but also the return on talent and other scarce resources.

Accordingly, an opportunity with a risk-adjusted present value of $100 million should take precedence over one of $20 million, assuming a similar return on capital and other resources. Without such a methodology, the tendency is to try to work on everything at once, which means nothing gets done quickly or well.

For example, if we were considering the purchase of a new manufacturing plant that was deficient in EH&S performance and operating management, we could accomplish significant improvement by transferring relevant talent from elsewhere inside Koch. But because there is always opportunity cost, we would need to conclude that the people would be more valuable in these new roles. True talent is a scarce resource. Its use needs to be carefully evaluated before being committed.

When setting priorities, one of the most difficult choices is between short-term optimization strategies and long-term growth and innovation strategies. The natural tendency is for a business to underinvest in long-term strategies. To offset this tendency it needs to commit dedicated resources to growth and innovation. Since long-term strategies won't result in profits for some time, incentives must be designed to reward progress in the interim (see chapter 10, "Incentives").

After vision-based priorities are set for the business as a whole, they must also be set for marketing, sales, operations (down to the plant level), supply, R&D, and support groups (especially those responsible for talent and culture). Each area must then assign responsibility for executing these priorities, based on what best advances the vision. Employees must then be held accountable for results.

Maximizing long-term value also involves creating experimental discovery processes that encourage new improvements, strategies, and innovations. When we are experimenting, we will have failures. As Einstein taught, "Someone who has never made a mistake has never tried anything new."[7] The key is to recognize when we are experimenting—and to ensure that our experiments reflect a reality-based vision.

Koch has been hurt as a company whenever we've failed to experiment prudently. Our losses in shipping in the 1970s and agriculture in the 1990s were costly examples of the failure to develop a reality-based vision and recognize that we did not have the capability to control experiments of such complexity and magnitude. It is worth noting that both of those businesses are profitable today, but only after being completely reconstituted.

In response to these failed, out-of-control experiments—such as our agriculture business trying to capture the "gas to bread spread" in the late 1990s—we developed new value-creating visions based on our actual capabilities. Koch Fertilizer has now realized its revised vision as a global fertilizer company that operates, markets, trades, and provides technology. This was made possible by the consistent, disciplined application of Market-Based Management. That same approach also allowed the Matador Cattle Company to make its revised vision a reality. Its Akaushi cattle produce delicious, heart-healthy beef that is much in demand. Although Koch Fertilizer and the Matador Cattle Company were once part of the failed Koch Agriculture Group, both are very successful businesses today.

We have learned that sustained, successful product development requires not only high-quality R&D, but a marketing and manufacturing organization that sees opportunities and has the capability, discipline, focus, resources, and culture to capture them. No matter what industry or industries you are in, innovation and integration are required throughout all of a company's business processes, from supply to manufacturing to marketing. Human resources, accounting, legal, compliance, and other support services have the same requirement.

OUR NORTH STAR

Koch's Vision benefits us in two ways: first as a set of fundamental principles that guide our behavior—a North Star—and second, as a strategic guide. In its role as a North Star, our Vision is a constant—it never changes. It is a compass to keep us going in the right direction rather than a destination we plan to reach.

It embodies fundamental principles, such as the role of business in society and our Guiding Principles. This articulation of our Vision is only modified as we learn to better explain these underlying principles.

In its role as a strategic guide, our Vision should change as the business environment and our capabilities change, and as we learn how to more effectively capture the best opportunities available to us.

To the extent that our Vision is realized, we will not only fulfill our role as a business, but further benefit society by motivating other companies to practice Principled Entrepreneurship such that they profit only by economic means. By educating and mobilizing key constituencies to advocate market-based policies that improve human well-being, together we can help people improve their lives through new and better jobs, new business opportunities, and safer communities in which people are mutually supportive. Surely this is a vision that everyone can embrace.

A company must have fundamental principles that guide behavior and a vision that enables it to create real value for its customers and in society. That's what good profit is all about.

CHAPTER 7

Virtue and Talents

VALUES FIRST

Winning takes talent; to repeat takes character.
—John Wooden[1]

Ten national college basketball championships in twelve years and a record eighty-eight-game winning streak. That's the best coaching record in the history of college basketball, and it belongs to the late John Wooden of UCLA. I don't believe his emphasis on character and his outstanding performance as a coach were coincidental. The best coaches place as much emphasis on virtue as on talent.

This is certainly true of Gregg Marshall, the coach of my hometown basketball team, the Wichita State Shockers. To ensure high school recruits have the right values, he doesn't just bring them to the campus and watch their behavior around their peers. He goes to their homes to visit with them and their parents. He tells me that if he detects too much arrogance at home, or a lack of respect for parents, he has an indication the recruit will not respond well to his highly disciplined coaching and emphasis on teamwork.

Wichita State usually can't attract the most talented players or best shooters—those get snatched up by the big-name basketball schools. And yet Coach Marshall took the Shockers to the Final

Four in the 2012–13 season and into the 2014 NCAA tournament undefeated, with a number one seed. His method of recruiting and coaching based on virtue is the reason why.

While we don't visit job applicants' homes, at Koch Industries we nonetheless screen for good character and compatible values during our first contact with a recruit. And we do so for every single person, no matter the job.

Over the telephone, our recruiters inquire into candidates' past behavior across a number of Guiding Principles. We are listening for behaviors such as how candidates have dealt with difficult situations in the past, whether or not they are respectful when speaking about others, if they are bureaucratic, or if they have difficulty admitting mistakes.

Moreover, when a candidate visits for an on-site interview, her interactions with the receptionist, strangers in the elevator, and cafeteria workers do not go unnoticed. Throughout the interview process we evaluate the candidate's behavior to determine if she is a good fit with our company's values.

Our interview process typically consists of a series of separate interviews, with each interviewer assessing a candidate's alignment with a unique set of personal traits. These traits are arranged as focus areas based on our Guiding Principles and are as follows: (1) Integrity and Compliance; (2) Value Creation, Principled Entrepreneurship, and Customer Focus; (3) Knowledge and Change; (4) Humility and Respect; and (5) Skills and Knowledge required in the role. Each interviewer has a focus area to cover and asks open-ended questions to discern a candidate's probability of success in demonstrating the desired traits. Once interviews are completed, a challenge session among the recruiter, interviewers, and hiring manager is held to ensure the best knowledge is shared when making a hiring determination.

This process has greatly improved our ability to select high-performing, long-term employees who behave in a manner consistent with our Guiding Principles.

While some companies focus exclusively on hiring individuals with the requisite skills for their openings and then hope these recruits possess aligned values, Koch transposes that approach. We focus *first* on values. It is our goal to fill every position with individuals who are equally virtuous and talented, but if forced to choose between one *or* the other, Koch will chose virtue every time. Why? Because we understand that talented people with bad values can do far more damage to a company than virtuous people with inferior talents.

If we happen to err (which is human) and hire someone with bad values, we better hope they also have a bad mind and work ethic. The worst employee is an energetic evil genius. Consider the fate of companies that only valued talent and neglected virtue: Enron, WorldCom, Barings Bank, and many more have fallen at the hands of fraud, corporate malfeasance, or some other employee scandal.

Our experience confirms that when a person has the appropriate values, beliefs, and intelligence, the needed skills and knowledge can usually be developed. Given the exceptional weight we place on alignment with our MBM Guiding Principles, it is sometimes difficult to find a candidate who also has the necessary skills. But it is much more difficult to change someone's values than to help them improve their knowledge.

An Ivy League–educated journalist from a famous New York business publication once interviewed me about Koch and our employees. The journalist probably meant no offense when she asked me, "Doesn't your location in Wichita make it hard to attract top talent?"

She was oblivious to the fact that Koch's location in the heartland is an asset, not a drawback. Anyone raised on farms knows the meaning of values and the importance of work ethic. If you decide to sleep instead of getting up to milk the cow one morning, you can't pass the buck or cover up your mistake. Other companies might prefer to interview applicants from Ivy League schools, but Koch has enjoyed much better results hiring from Wichita State or

Kansas State than from Harvard. (The four employees who have succeeded me as president of Koch Industries hailed from the Murray State University School of Agriculture, Texas A&M, the University of Tulsa, and Emporia State University.)

Every organization has its own culture. If that culture is not created consciously and purposively, it will degenerate into a cult of personality or an "anything goes" environment. Whether good or bad, an organization's culture is determined by the values, beliefs, and conduct of its members, as well as the rules and incentives set by its leaders—and modeled by them behaviorally. Koch's core values are incorporated in our MBM Guiding Principles and our Code of Conduct, which experience convinces us are critical for good profit in the long term.

MBM requires a culture with many virtues that, fortunately, can frequently be cultivated if they are underdeveloped in new hires. (To be sure, some can't be implanted if they are missing.) These attributes set the standards for evaluating policies and practices, measuring conduct, and establishing the norms of behavior and shared values and beliefs that guide individual actions. But it's important to recognize that *they are guidelines, not specific orders.*

Setting expectations according to general principles rather than specific orders not only helps employees understand the importance of their work; it frees them to think and innovate. We've experienced little progress when our people mindlessly followed instructions—whether they had good values or not.

I entered the business world with an inquisitive mind molded by a science background and a longtime distaste for blindly following orders. Any group of people, whether a society or an organization, functions more effectively when guided by general rules of just conduct rather than specific commands. As the French writer Frédéric Bastiat observed: "The surest way to have the laws respected is to make them respectable."[2] Leaving the particulars to those doing the work encourages discovery and enhances their ability to adapt to changing conditions.

In his "The Republic of Science," Polanyi writes, "Thus the

authority of scientific opinion enforces the teachings of science in general, for the very purpose of fostering their subversion in the particular."[3] In business, this means setting certain standards (in Koch's case, our Guiding Principles). Freeing people to explore new approaches within these standards leads to innovation. Furthermore, applying the law of scientific proof (looking for evidence that disproves our proposition with the same diligence that we look for evidence that supports it) is crucial to innovation. The best scientists are humble and intellectually honest. And the environment in which they can best explore is one based on the principles of a free society.

Unless Koch remains humble, our company will be caught off guard by creative destruction. We must never think of ourselves as too big—or too good—to fail. To get the full benefit of MBM, all employees must internalize our core values and exemplify them in everything they do.

Those values, which Koch refers to as its Guiding Principles, are drawn from three different realms. The first is the underlying framework of the free society, where innovation and productivity thrive—to the degree that the framework is upheld. The second category is the theories of philosophers and psychologists whose behavioral prescriptions strike me as refreshingly reality-based—thinkers such as Hayek, Polanyi, and Maslow.

The third is my own life experience, which was spent working with all different kinds of people. I've been honored to have worked with many with the right kind of values, most notably my father, and Sterling Varner. But there were many others I was exposed to whose values I questioned: my Centennial Valley bunkmate Bitterroot Bob; my classmates back in Quanah who were mystified as to why I did more than the minimum needed to pass a math exam; the Communist revolutionaries who promised heaven on earth but delivered hell; the business leaders who hurt so many Americans when they promised riches but delivered bankruptcy; and the U.S. politicians who promised to eliminate poverty but made it permanent instead.

I am not a perfect exemplar of ideal values. (Remember me trying to cut ahead in a disorganized line for movie tickets, and slacking off at MIT before my father threatened to stop paying my tuition?) No one is born with the right values, myself included. I had to *learn* the principles that are important for success in business, and how they are best articulated and applied. Everyone, in every business, and in every position within a company, can be constantly learning and strengthening the values that drive good profit.

Every year, I am subjected to the same kind of evaluation that is done throughout Koch—an evaluation of my performance by those I work with most closely. I want to know how to increase my contributions—and I get some great suggestions. (More on that later.)

GUIDING PRINCIPLES IN ACTION

Maintaining and enhancing the most beneficial culture at Koch requires every employee—including the CEO—to internalize and practice these Guiding Principles.

> MBM GUIDING PRINCIPLES
> 1. Integrity
> 2. Compliance
> 3. Value creation
> 4. Principled entrepreneurship
> 5. Customer focus
> 6. Knowledge
> 7. Change
> 8. Humility
> 9. Respect
> 10. Fulfillment

Here is a summary of these principles in practice.

1. Integrity: Ours is a system for ethical people. It will work for no other, to paraphrase John Adams.[4] And that's how it is at Koch. Integrity is critically important for MBM. Conducting all affairs with integrity is our first principle because it is the basis for trust and the foundation for mutually beneficial relations with all our constituencies—employees, customers, suppliers, partners, communities, and governments.

Imagine how productive business would be if everyone acted with complete integrity, with their word as their bond, never doing anything they wouldn't want exposed to the whole world. There would be much less need for all the time and money spent on controls, contracts, litigation, and security, and the enormous drag of transaction costs would be greatly reduced.

At Koch, integrity means firm adherence to a moral code, outlined in our Guiding Principles and Code of Conduct. It requires courage, because acting in harmony with our principles can cause discomfort and fear—especially when it involves challenging conventional wisdom. But what good are principles if we abandon them under pressure?

2. Compliance: Second only to integrity is compliance, emphasized by our "10,000 percent" goal of 100 percent of employees fully complying 100 percent of the time. We have seen how it takes only one person doing the wrong thing, one time, to do irreparable harm in society, to the company, and to fellow employees.

Company principles and policies are established with a twofold goal: to ensure that employees comply with the law—whether they agree with it or not—and that their practices are supportive of the company's long-term success. If something seems off, employees are supposed to "Stop, think, and ask."

A good example of this occurred in 2011, when the leaders of Georgia-Pacific's gypsum business noticed that many of its competitors in the wallboard market were sending customers price announcements that were noticeably different from those in the past, with content that could give rise to accusations of "price-fixing." The gypsum business management team worked with Georgia-Pacific's legal and compliance officers to make sure that GP's own pricing was clearly independent and announced in a way that couldn't be misconstrued as violating antitrust law.

Sure enough, a state attorney general's office soon began investigating gypsum drywall pricing—but GP was able to provide them with ample documentation of its innocence.

Predictably, private plaintiffs' lawsuits against the U.S. gypsum wallboard industry followed. While GP was originally named as a defendant, after it shared its records with plaintiffs' counsel that demonstrated its clear lack of involvement in any potential antitrust violation, GP was ultimately not named as a defendant. GP's regard for the Guiding Principles, especially Principles 1 and 2 (Integrity and Compliance), saved Koch untold hours of costly litigation and prevented damage to our reputation.

All employees—especially those with long histories at other companies where compliance amounts to lip service—must accept the responsibility to manage the requirements and risks associated with their roles. This can only be accomplished by holding everyone involved accountable, especially those in the management chain. "But I was unaware" is not an excuse.

3. **Value Creation:** As chapter 6 explained, our vision is to create long-term value by economic means for customers, society, and the company. Customers come first in this list because without them there is no business. Creating value by "economic means" also requires that our actions are beneficial for our communities and others in society.

Applying MBM helps employees make better decisions, enhance safety and environmental excellence, eliminate waste, optimize, and innovate—all of which contribute to value creation. Our commitment to these principles goes beyond compliance. For us, protecting people is paramount. While minor injuries or environmental issues are unacceptable and must be avoided, if one single thing takes priority, it is eliminating the risk of a catastrophic event, especially fatalities. Preventing serious injuries (and even the near misses, which in slightly different circumstances would have caused grave harm) is our top priority.

Some see conservation and profit as being at odds with one another. But when understood through the lens of our Guiding Principles, it becomes clear that they are, in fact, in harmony. Creative destruction necessitates that we discover better ways not only to create value for customers, but to eliminate waste and minimize the use of resources in order to create superior long-term results.

This is well illustrated by Koch's John Zink Hamworthy Combustion subsidiary, which has designed a profitable system that captures the gas from industry flaring during upsets and converts it into fuel or feedstock. This process essentially eliminates the need for flaring (emergencies and scheduled maintenance notwithstanding) and reduces emissions that compromise air quality and waste money.

Creative destruction, as demonstrated by this example, points us toward the culture of innovation and entrepreneurship covered in the next principle.

4. Principled Entrepreneurship: This principle—so central to our culture that we had it trademarked—is defined as "maximizing the long-term profitability of the business by creating superior value for our customers while consuming fewer resources and always acting lawfully and with integrity." Creating value for society requires Principled Entrepreneurship—not political or other forms of entrepreneurship, such as corporate welfare or fraud.

We expect employees to apply judgment, responsibility, initiative, economic and critical thinking skills, and the sense of urgency necessary to generate the greatest contribution, consistent with the company's risk philosophy (more on this shortly).

Judgment is the process of forming an opinion, evaluating

alternatives, or selecting a course of action by discerning and comparing.

Responsibility includes two important ideas—choosing right over wrong and accepting ownership for one's conduct and obligations. Employees are responsible and must be held accountable for their behavior and results.

Initiative means thinking and acting without being urged, and originating new ideas or methods.

Economic thinking skills are developed by learning our concepts (such as opportunity cost, comparative advantage, etc.) and tools, and then applying them to get results. They should lead to an ability to identify and frame important issues in a way that helps us decide on the most profitable course of action.

Critical thinking skills involve looking beyond the obvious to anticipate second- and third-order effects. They are essential for innovation.

Urgency is necessary if we are to improve at a faster rate than our competitors. This is accomplished by eliminating steps and activities that don't add sufficient value to justify the time and expense involved, considering opportunity cost.

Lastly, employees need to make decisions that reflect the *company's* risk philosophy rather than their own. Any approach to business risk involves both risk preference (one's inherent inclination toward or away from risk) and risk tolerance (the magnitude of risk that one finds acceptable).

In general, since the company makes numerous financial bets and has far greater resources, the company's risk philosophy differs markedly from any individual employee's. For the company to continue to be successful and grow, employees must undertake far higher and larger financial risks than they would as individuals, so long as it is compliant and profitable to do so.

Consider this example: Should an employee work on an investment with a 90 percent chance of making $100,000 rather than one with a 50 percent chance of making $1 million? No, because on a risk-adjusted basis, the company makes only $90,000 rather than $500,000. In order to earn the better profit, we need employees to overcome the aversion many of them have to taking a significant chance their efforts will yield nothing.

5. Customer Focus: Developing long-lasting relationships with customers and suppliers has been a key part of our success and theirs. It requires win-win relationships based on aligned visions, values, and incentives, and a strong foundation of earned trust.

Like England's King George VI, Sterling Varner often stammered when he spoke. (The comparison may end there, as Sterling was born in a tent in Ranger, Texas, never finished college, and worked with mules delivering oilfield equipment.) That stammer caused him to talk less and listen more. Perhaps as a result, Sterling was as good at developing customer relationships as anyone I've ever known. To generate good profit, it's critical not only to understand but to anticipate what customers value, their expectations, measures, incentives, needs, alternatives, and decision-making processes.

Sterling's ability with customers helped Koch toward its objective of becoming a preferred supplier. Anyone can do that by developing the kind of relationships with customers that build trust, anticipating their needs, and going beyond what they know and say. As discussed in the previous chapter, reacting to customers' demonstrated preference is important, but we must do more. It is impossible for customers to truly know what they would prefer to their current alternatives until they know what will become available. Mobile phone customers didn't anticipate they would want devices to text message or to locate the best pizza joint in a five-block radius—the phones' developers did.

6. Knowledge: Seek and use the best knowledge and proactively share your knowledge while welcoming challenges. Measures should guide action and create knowledge, leading to better decisions, innovation, and profitable action.

At Koch we evaluate all measures against this principle and

strive to develop and use the critical few that help us improve. We encourage employees to proactively seek out the best sources of useful knowledge—inside and outside the company—rather than being satisfied with familiar sources. Think of how Flint Hills' and INVISTA's plants may benefit from the knowledge of the sensor technology Molex is developing, or how Molex is benefiting from knowledge of the market for sensors provided by Georgia-Pacific. We enthusiastically encourage this kind of cross-company knowledge sharing. It is particularly important for everyone to embrace a challenge culture, both by soliciting different perspectives and expertise, and by having the courage to constructively speak up when we disagree.

Because all progress and well-being comes from superior development and application of knowledge, the principle of knowledge sharing is more fully developed in the next chapter.

7. **Change:** Significant competitive advantages accrue to those who are the first to foresee change and act quickly on that foresight. Equivalent benefits accrue to those who drive creative destruction through pervasive continual experimentation.

Experimental discovery is needed because we cannot know the final destination when our journey begins. Innovation usually involves numerous changes in direction that lead to the discovery of new paths. (Remember, neither Christopher Columbus nor Lewis and Clark found what they were looking for, but in the process of looking they made discoveries of enormous importance.) A good experiment leads to new knowledge that brings about change, even if our assumptions or hypotheses turn out to be wrong. Of course, the magnitude of resources invested in an experiment should be determined by the probability of success and the potential benefit.

8. **Humility:** Arrogance is one of the most destructive traits in an organization. It hurts productivity by causing people to be oblivious to their own limitations and the contributions of others.

The destructiveness of pride is so great it led Pope Gregory in A.D. 590 to list it as one of the seven deadly sins.

We all need to exemplify humility and intellectual honesty as vital attributes in our culture. To create value, we must all constantly seek to understand and constructively deal with reality to create value and achieve personal improvement.

Having humility means understanding and accepting yourself as you really are. It means admitting your mistakes and what you don't know rather than being defensive and blaming others. Intellectual honesty takes humility to the next level. It is dedication to truth—no matter how painful. It is sincerely seeking constructive criticism, not what Somerset Maugham identified as the more usual human tendency: "People ask you for criticism, but they only want praise."[5]

Holding ourselves and others accountable also requires courage and intellectual honesty, especially when we are faced with the unpleasant task of dealing with the performance or behavior issues of a coworker. A culture that lacks accountability lacks integrity and cannot survive, let alone thrive.

9. **Respect:** For a business to be successful over the long term, it must respect the customer and what she values. With more than 100,000 employees and a presence in sixty-four countries, we rely on diversity—and respect for differences—to help us better understand and relate to customers, suppliers, and communities everywhere. We make every effort to recruit broadly, so as to find those who can create the most value through a diversity of ability, knowledge, skills, perspectives, and experience.

Treating people based on their individual merits—not according to race, religion, sex, or any other grouping—is not only the foundation of a free society; it is the right thing to do. Similarly, organizations should treat people as individuals, according to their virtue, talents, and contributions. Teamwork requires honesty, dignity, respect, and sensitivity. Making people feel appreciated leads to better long-term results. If we mistreat our coworkers, they won't cooperate or communicate openly and honestly, and we lose their trust, knowledge, and commitment.

Not having the courage to give honest feedback is a disservice to both the individual and the company. Dishonesty in our dealings constitutes a breach in integrity and fails the test of respect, because it usually leads to a bad outcome for the individual. How can anyone improve if not given critical feedback?

As Maslow pointed out, this feedback must be given in a manner that is not considered an attack on or rejection of the person. For feedback to be constructive, the person delivering it must have previously proven that he respects and cares for, and is trying to help, the other person.

10. Fulfillment: No company can succeed if its employees just put in their time and daydream about what they are going to do after work. At Koch, we look for people who work with such intensity and passion they even wake up at night with ideas. When we fully develop our potential, we create superior value for others— and that in turn helps give meaning to our lives.

We cannot ignite a passion for creating the greatest value if there is no meaning in our work. Life is pretty empty without passion for what we are doing. What a tragedy to reach the end of your life and only be able to say, "I got by without having to do too much."

WALKING THE TALK

Although these principles may seem commonsensical, developing the ability to apply them routinely and instinctively to achieve results requires constant reflection and practice. As Voltaire noted, common sense is not so common.[6]

Many companies have principles somewhat similar to Koch's

Guiding Principles, but rarely are they the basis for a company's culture. Very few companies take a systematic approach to making them central to every aspect of employment. Failing to do so ensures that the principles become nothing more than empty slogans, buzzwords, or posters on the walls, with managers often widely viewed as hypocrites.

At Koch we strive to hire and retain only those who embrace our principles. We give detailed explanations of our Guiding Principles and their role (investing a great deal of time and resources in mentoring and training), and clearly and consistently communicate the expectation that these principles guide employee behavior.

We ensure that opportunities, advancement, and compensation depend on how well an employee reflects our Guiding Principles. We also give regular feedback and will ultimately terminate employees who do not act in harmony with them. That's how serious we are about ensuring our culture is based on principles.

For MBM to be applied effectively, *results must be the focus*. The challenge is to get beyond the superficial stage in which employees understand the words and concepts but haven't yet been able to effectively apply them. Promoting those who cannot "walk the talk" undermines our ability to create value and damages the culture. Like chess players, we must apply the concepts and basic rules in a way that creates winning strategies. A key talent for leaders is the ability to identify people who are able to apply these principles to achieve superior results.

Whether or not you work for a company with guiding principles as explicitly codified as Koch's, leaders should be selected from among those who have not only demonstrated the ability to understand and apply these principles, but who are positive role models for workplace culture. Because leaders set the standard—both by how they lead and by what they do—they are the guardians of, and must be held accountable for, the culture. To be effective, leaders must internalize and consistently apply those principles in a way that produces results.

Creating a beneficial culture is impossible without mentoring and positive examples. At Koch, good leaders not only live by our Guiding Principles; they regularly review them with all employees. In any company, the most effective leaders are those who provide frequent and honest feedback that identifies opportunities for improvement in a way that stimulates dialogue and change. They hold themselves, their employees, peers, and management accountable.

The importance of culture and leadership are well illustrated by another great coach, Jack Clark, the rugby coach at the University of California. To my knowledge, Jack has the best long-term record in intercollegiate sports. In his thirty-one years as coach he has won twenty-two national championships. For him, as for us, culture is key:

> We as a team are our values. We use them daily as a touchstone to help inform every decision we make. We process every piece of team operations through these beliefs. We are indeed grateful and truly believe we are not owed a thing. Our team always comes first and this fact informs every strategy and policy. Getting better, improving, is the driving force within the team. We cherish merit and celebrate toughness. We believe leadership is an ability and responsibility for all. Our definition of leadership is the ability to make those around you better and more productive.[7]

RECRUITING FOR TALENT, TOO

Although employees should be selected and retained, first and foremost, on the basis of their values and beliefs, they must also have the talent necessary to produce results. Employees with insufficient virtue have done far more damage to companies than those with insufficient talent, but virtue without the required talent does not create value.

⅄ ⅄ ⅄

To recruit the talent necessary for achieving our vision, we try to anticipate the future needs of the company and continually search for candidates who, in addition to demonstrating virtue, demonstrate the abilities to perform at a superior level.

Instead of only hiring when we have an open position, we attempt to hire talented people when we identify them—even when we don't have an obvious, immediate opening. We recognize that they will find a way to create superior value, and therefore the risk is justified.

To identify sufficient candidates who meet our requirements, we encourage all employees to recommend external talent, and employee referrals have resulted in some of our best hires. We also have developed strategic relationships with external sources, including search firms familiar with MBM and our Guiding Principles.

To help satisfy our increasing demand for talent, we have transformed our college recruiting efforts. A critical aspect of this transformation has been a well-developed internship program, which allows Koch to evaluate the real person—and not just a résumé—before making a job offer.

Through this program, the intern and the company get to know each other very well. We allow interns to do valuable work rather than "busy work," which benefits them as well as us. We tend to recruit interns at universities where we have relationships through scholarships and other programs. This helps us identify interns who fit our Guiding Principles. As a result, about 70 percent of Koch interns become full-time employees—compared to a national average of 50 percent.

We have found it is relatively easy for recruits right out of school to learn our culture. Learning the culture is much more difficult for new hires from companies with antithetical cultures, where playing politics or navigating a maze of detailed, bureaucratic rules was necessary for a successful career. In general, those who have risen the highest in those kinds of organizations seem to struggle the most at Koch.

Replacing old mental models with new ones based on our Guiding Principles is no easy task. It takes a real desire to change on the employee's part as well as patience and mentoring by the company. But until employees make that transformation, we don't get the full benefit of their knowledge and talent, and they get less fulfillment working at Koch.

No matter how difficult the role is to fill, it is critical that we not lower our standards. A bad hiring decision is much more costly in many, many ways than is the delay in finding the right candidate.

PUTTING THEM BOTH TOGETHER

To evaluate a candidate's or employee's fit with our requirement for both virtue and talents, Koch—true to its engineering roots—uses a matrix.

As shown in the diagram on the opposite page, the vertical axis is a subjective measure of the individual's fit with the desired values and beliefs. The horizontal axis reflects our assessment of the skills and knowledge required for that individual's role.

Quadrant I of the matrix represents the expectation for an employee. Many employees new to a role will initially be in quadrant II, but this should be a temporary situation. If an employee is in III or IV, we recognize we made a mistake and do not retain him, unless we believe his problem is caused by lack of understanding, and he quickly demonstrates his willingness to modify his behavior.

An employee who, for whatever reason, is not in quadrant I is expected to get there quickly. We expect all employees and candidates to align their behavior with the values and beliefs expressed in our MBM Guiding Principles. Employees also must have the potential to build the requisite skills and knowledge to meet or exceed the expectations of their roles and responsibilities. Supe-

VIRTUE AND TALENTS MATRIX

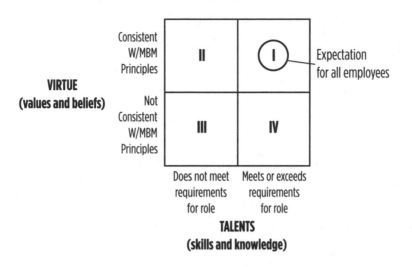

rior capabilities cannot exist without talent that generates superior performance. That's where Koch's Talent Management Process comes in.

DESIGNING ROLES TO FIT

I believe that a person's capacity to perform in a given role is not only determined by training and experience, but by the aptitude or the kinds of intelligences in which that person excels. Our Talent Management Process helps determine the best-fitting role for each individual employee by using Harvard psychologist Howard Gardner's theory of multiple intelligences.[8]

Gardner's theory postulates that there are eight different kinds of intelligence, and none of us is equally gifted or deficient in all of them. These are: interpersonal, intrapersonal, linguistic, logical-mathematical, spatial, naturalist, bodily-kinesthetic, and musical.

This underutilized model is critically important for an organization because, when internalized, it helps leaders better apply the concept of comparative advantage. People's potential to develop specific skills and knowledge is determined by their individual intelligences. Thus performance increases markedly whenever roles (a combination of responsibilities) are designed to fit employees' individual aptitudes. (See "Roles, Responsibilities, and Expectations" in chapter 9, "Decision Rights.")

Consider the example of Michael Jordan. He established himself as one of the greatest basketball players ever, yet he also wanted to play baseball. When he failed at that, he returned to basketball and was tremendously successful in the role that fit his natural ability.

Pre-existing "job descriptions" waste an organization's resources by trying to fit square pegs into round holes and vice versa. Koch is able to create more value for customers and society, and offer more fulfillment, by developing individualized roles, responsibilities, and expectations that value and fully utilize employees' natural abilities.

To maximize long-term profitability, each employee—whether long-term or newly hired—must be committed to sound principles, have the appropriate level and kind of talent, and perform in the optimum role.

TALENT PLANNING

To assess the overall strength of talent in an organization, we use a Talent Planning process we call "ABC ratings." Leaders are asked to assess each of their employees' comparative advantages, development, opportunities, and readiness for next assignments, and then assign their performances a letter grade: A, B, or C.

This process is very different from the forced ranking that some companies use—separating the bottom 10 percent of their employees every year, like a professor determined to fail the bottom tenth of her class even if those students actually performed passably. (I remember receiving a 45/100 on a college physics test and worrying that I'd flunked this incomprehensible course. But since the average grade was in the 20s, I wound up with an A on the curve.)

Our goal is for all our employees to be high performers—not to pit them against each other. No employee has to receive a C, and for those who do, an attempt should be made to give them the help and training they need to improve.

These grades are assigned using the following guidelines:

A Level

Performance and contribution in a role that provides a significant competitive advantage over similar roles at principal competitors and, therefore, is an exceptional contributor to long-term profitability. Employees at this level of performance usually represent the top 15 percent of peers in their industry. Our businesses and capabilities constantly seek to hire As and ensure we don't lose them. Koch is always in the market for employees capable of A-level performance and continually strives to improve its ability to identify, recruit, retain, and motivate these competitively advantaged individuals.

B Level

Performance and contribution in a role that has proven to be at least as good as that of peers at principal competitors. While not in the top tier, it is in the top half of performers in the industry. B-level performance is solid and consistently meets and may even exceed expectations in many areas of performance. Employees performing at this level are, collectively, critical to a company's success. They are not an afterthought, living in the shadow of A performers; however, they should be challenged to grow and improve.

C Level

Performance and contribution in a role that puts the company at a competitive disadvantage by being below average relative to peers at principal competitors. C-level performance does not meet expectations. The employee may be in the wrong role, meaning he could contribute at a B or even an A level if he were in a role that better leveraged his comparative advantages. But if his performance cannot be improved to a B level, either by finding a suitable role or through development, he should not be retained.

As Gardner's theory indicates, an employee's inability to create value in a given role does not mean the employee couldn't do so in a different role. In fact, in many cases the opposite is true. So the next step after the evaluation is to determine if the deficiency in performance is caused simply by the individual being in the wrong role. Michael Jordan might have been a B or C in baseball, but he was certainly an A in basketball.

Likewise, inability to create value at one company does not mean the same will be true elsewhere. Employees may be much more successful in another organization that has needs or a culture better suited to their talents and virtue.

The purpose of the ABC process is not to elevate or stigmatize anyone, but to ensure we are attracting, hiring, developing, placing, and retaining the talent we need to succeed in the long term. This is why we discourage disclosure of these ratings.

No matter what process you choose to adopt for assessing talent, it should not be applied as a bureaucratic, rigid formula. Instead, it should be used as a tool to identify employees capable of A-level performance, detect any failures by management in dealing with C-level performances, and assist employees in the wrong roles to find better ones. Leadership should act quickly to close gaps so that the performance of the organization can improve.

Of course, employee performance will vary over time. Some employees will greatly improve their performance over months and years, while others may be unable to adapt to a changing environment or other factors. Since employees can change with their circumstances, it is important to evaluate them regularly and apply the A, B, or C ratings to their current performance—not to how they performed in the past. The rating is not an immutable measure of the value they can create; it is a measure of the value they are creating now.

Attracting as much A-level talent as possible enables a business to build additional capabilities and competitive advantages, capture more growth opportunities, and provide for succession. We have missed a number of opportunities because we didn't have the necessary talent available. So we now take a more proactive approach by hiring those we think have the potential to add superior value, regardless of whether they can fill an existing role.

What we do is different from building "bench strength." Our A performers don't sit on the bench. When we hire A performers without a position open, we make it a point to give them the opportunity to create real value. There are always more opportunities than there are people to capture them, so it pays to constantly supplement internal talent.

PERFORMANCE DEVELOPMENT

When poor performance is not addressed (including allowing poor performers to stay in their roles—especially leadership roles), an organization inevitably becomes dysfunctional. For a performance management process to be effective, it must address these problems. It cannot allow supervisors to just go through the motions when giving feedback, failing to honestly force the employee to face shortcomings in his performance.

To deal with the tendency for supervisors to avoid unpleasant conversations with their employees, feedback should be designed to actually help employees improve their performance. Such feedback should be specific, direct, and honest, rather than general, vague, and comforting. It needs to be factual, using self-assessment and 360-degree input from those who have worked with the employee most closely. At Koch, we find this approach is much more effective than the widely used formulaic ratings that are easier to administer.

Koch gives employees feedback on three main areas: major contributions, strengths, and improvement areas. By listing specific examples of contributions to the company, we encourage employees to strive to do even more of the same. Summarizing key strengths provides the knowledge to ensure employees' roles fit their comparative advantages.

For our qualitative approach to be successful, supervisors must be clear about strengths and development needs—especially when an employee is not meeting expectations. For employees to improve, the supervisor must have the courage to tell them what they need to work on.

At the same time, employees must be open and receptive to honest feedback. (New employees often comment that this is the first time they have gotten the kind of direct feedback that will actually help them improve their performance. While it can be a little hard to take, it is very beneficial.)

This process focuses both the employee and the supervisor on improving performance. And don't forget that *all* of us have room to improve—even CEOs. Here are some of the improvement recommendations contained in my February 2015 performance evaluation:

- "Avoid sending mixed signals on risk-taking."
- "Consistently give feedback to responses on your information requests."
- "Keep analyses focused on accuracy rather than precision."

I find my annual performance review to be very constructive. CEOs must be as open and receptive to honest feedback as any other employee. Would we rather have our egos bruised a little by tough feedback, or bruised big time by a major failure?

CAREER DEVELOPMENT

Consistent with our MBM philosophy, Koch employees are expected to think and act like principled entrepreneurs and take ownership of their careers. They must be willing to share their career aspirations and seek feedback in developing realistic career goals. This gives supervisors at all levels essential knowledge and helps the company optimize its talent pool.

By developing their individual capabilities, employees make a greater contribution, find greater fulfillment in their work, and are more likely to reach their maximum potential. Instead of using centralized curricula or rigid career paths (which cannot take into account individual needs, abilities, and preferences), we strive to provide an internal marketplace for employees, making career choices available to them based on their aptitude and interests, while taking into account how they can make the greatest contribution to the company.

Supervisors, with support from HR, are expected to assist in this development process. They do so by identifying performance gaps, providing feedback, coaching, modifying current roles to better fit capabilities, and preparing employees for new roles. Supervisors are responsible for the career development of the individuals on their team and for maintaining a culture that maximizes employee development and eliminates talent hoarding. This requires that supervisors offer their employees opportunities that become available in other parts of Koch. If they don't, the talent pool won't be optimized, morale will suffer, and we will lose high-potential employees.

People sometimes believe that to advance their careers, promotions and other role changes are required. We strive to make this unnecessary, so they can remain focused on creating value rather than on their next move.

When supervisors keep employees engaged and develop their skills, increases in responsibilities, contributions, and compensation will follow. Employees perform much better when they can maximize their contributions without regard for promotions, job titles, or some predetermined path forward.

On-the-job coaching is the most effective way to help employees develop in any kind of company. Formal training can impart basic knowledge to employees, and ours emphasizes compliance, ethics, and MBM concepts and tools. (Our MBM Capability, described in chapter 4, is good at making the theoretical practical for employees.) But training is no substitute for mentored work experience, so we place more value on the supervisor-employee relationship than on training.

Effective individual development benefits both the employee and the company. Employees prosper and find greater fulfillment in their work, while the company satisfies a basic requirement for long-term success: the development, retention, and motivation of highly productive employees.

When I contacted Coach Clark to ask his permission to quote him in this book, he graciously consented. He wrote back, "We believe our values are best accessed through this mind-set: Grateful for everything; entitled to nothing."[9]

The old cliché is true: Good people are a company's most valuable resource. They are also essential for good profit. I join Jack Clark in feeling grateful for everything and entitled to nothing. I am especially grateful for all our good people.

CHAPTER 8

Knowledge Processes

USING INFORMATION TO PRODUCE

RESULTS

*It is one thing to wish to have truth on our side, and
another thing to wish sincerely to be on the side of truth.*
—RICHARD WHATELY[1]

My three brothers and I have something in common that I would not wish upon any man: prostate cancer. David's case was the most severe.

It was already at an advanced stage when it was discovered in 1992. After undergoing unsuccessful radiation followed by surgery, he married for the first time at age fifty-six and had three children with his wife, Julia. But the cancer came back, and no medical treatment yet has been able to eradicate it permanently. Hormone therapy has thus far kept the cancer at bay. Scrambling as fast as possible, for as much knowledge as possible, from the best possible sources, has kept David alive for over two decades.

As my father foretold, adversity can often be a blessing in disguise. Because of his diagnosis and experience with the shortcomings of various therapies, David has become a passionate leader in the funding of cancer research, for the benefit of all. One of his most significant cancer treatment gifts established an institute at MIT whose mission is "to develop new insights into cancer as well as new tools and technologies to better treat, diagnose and prevent cancer." It stands to reason that David—born with an engineer's mind—would care deeply about the search for the best tools and technologies to fight this vicious disease.

The institute's lab space and common areas were specifically designed to foster interaction and a culture of collaboration between engineers and scientists. Using an interdisciplinary approach, the institute brings biologists and chemists together with computer scientists, clinicians, and biological, chemical, mechanical, and materials science engineers. It is called the David H. Koch Institute for Integrative Cancer Research at MIT—or the Koch Institute, for short. To my mind, its organizing principle makes it an exemplar of one of the five dimensions necessary for good profit: knowledge processes.

Knowledge processes are derived from a structure and a culture that enable participants to innovate by spontaneously sharing discoveries, just as they do at the Koch Institute. This chapter is about how you can create an innovative organization through knowledge sharing as well.

SPONTANEOUS KNOWLEDGE SHARING

The Koch Institute's research is focused on five programs viewed as critical for rapid progress toward controlling cancer: (1) developing nanotechnology-based cancer therapeutics; (2) creating novel devices for cancer detection and monitoring; (3) exploring the molecular and cellular basis of metastasis; (4) advancing personalized medicine through systematic analysis of cancer pathways and drug resistance linked to individual cancers; and (5) engineering the immune system to fight cancer.

The institute's merging of technologies, disciplines, and approaches in each of these areas, traditionally viewed as distinct, creates a host of new opportunities. By bringing together engineering, physical sciences, and life sciences, the Koch Institute is poised to make significant breakthroughs in overcoming the terrible blight of cancer.

Whether the goal is to cure cancer, build a smaller and faster smartphone, or develop a more efficient and environmentally friendly way of making nylon, disruptive innovation requires creating, acquiring, sharing, and applying knowledge. The methods used to do so are what we at Koch call knowledge processes. They include mechanisms to inform us immediately about developments everywhere in the world, and measures that give us feedback on how to improve our vision and mark our progress based on the best information and discoveries.

When Liz and I visited the institute with Julia and David for its dedication, there were tears in David's eyes throughout much of the ceremony. Just as moving for me was the realization that the biologists and engineers at the institute were using what is probably the most effective methodology against any intractable problem—Polanyi's "Republic of Science," a well-read copy of which I keep in my credenza.

In that work, the chemistry professor-turned-philosopher envisioned a "society of explorers" striving "towards an unknown future." The research center that now stands in Cambridge, Massachusetts, is a human life–valuing embodiment of that vision—a place teeming with intelligence and dedication, housed in a remarkable building made possible by my younger brother.

The Koch Institute, formed along the lines of Polanyi's vision, confirms for me that those who seek excellence—whether in science, business, sports, the arts, or other pursuits—naturally gravitate toward this approach, which is a type of knowledge process.

"We have clustered together the very best scientists and engineers, all with their sights trained on a distant and still-indistinct goal," explained Dr. Susan Hockfield, MIT's president when the Koch Institute opened. "While we leave them to self-direct their research, we have confidence that their community intelligence and leaps of insight will be greater than what any of these brilliant individuals could accomplish on their own."[2]

Polanyi, I think, would agree. The scientific community is innovative because it provides "a framework of discipline and at the same time [encourages] rebellion against it," he wrote. (This also describes my adolescence well, and could be one reason I'm drawn to the sciences.) It "enforces the teachings of science in general for the very purpose of fostering their subversion in [the] particular."

The Koch Institute uncannily matches Polanyi's description of spontaneous order—of mutually adjusting individual initiatives, through shared knowledge. If one thinks of the cancer problem as a puzzle, the following passage by Polanyi reads like instructions for finding its cure:

> Imagine that we are given the pieces of a very large jigsaw puzzle, and suppose that for some reason it is important that our giant puzzle be put together in the shortest possible time. We would naturally try to speed this up by engaging a number of helpers; the question is in what manner these could be best employed. The only way the assistants can effectively cooperate, and surpass by far what any single one of them could do, is to let them work on putting the puzzle together in sight of the others so that every time a piece of it is fitted in by one helper, all the others will immediately watch out for the next step that becomes possible in consequence. Under this system, each helper will act on his own initiative, by responding to the latest achievements of the others, and the completion of their joint task will be greatly accelerated. We have here in a nutshell the way in which a series of independent initiatives are organized to a joint achievement by mutually adjusting themselves at every successive stage to the situation created by all the others who are acting likewise.[3]

For a culture—whether that culture is found in a state-of-the-art research center, a multinational organization, or a fledgling start-up—to create a spontaneous order that contributes to discovery, it must constantly seek, nurture, and implement new knowledge. Not every organization exhibits these virtuous qualities. That's why in MBM, the Virtue and Talents dimension is interdependent with Knowledge Processes—because it takes a certain kind of person who is willing to collaborate. (Of course, all five dimensions are interdependent, something we stress at Koch as we apply them holistically.)

The resulting culture is the opposite of one in which workers blindly follow marching orders. Instead of a set of directions, we provide employees an environment and a toolbox. Every employee works with his supervisor to develop a role, responsibilities, and expectations. Ideas are encouraged and challenged, not destructively criticized. The kind of communication that fosters value creation requires constructive disagreement.

Anyone who wants to maximize creativity should work as part of interdisciplinary teams, sharing ideas as people do at the Koch Institute—not in isolated silos—and their leaders must provide them sufficient resources and time to do so. People must also make time by recognizing the opportunity cost of less important work. Dedicating a full-time, A-level performer to a particularly thorny problem is often the key to successful innovation.

By 2004, INVISTA had abandoned formal plans to develop a new process for a key ingredient in nylon production due to several seemingly insurmountable technical barriers. After we acquired INVISTA, we supported its research leader in allowing his team to continue working on the process.

Two years later, they achieved a game-changing breakthrough. The leader quickly won approval for laboratory testing and a pilot program. At this point, his strong talent for bringing technologies from "paper to piloting" was needed to build new biotechnology capabilities from scratch. So he switched roles to lead the creation of a world-class biotechnology center in the UK, which, again, has achieved extraordinary breakthroughs in a short period of time.

To take the new nylon process from the pilot stage to the

commercial stage required another A-level R&D leader. So another talented INVISTA scientist, with both manufacturing and commercial experience, led the team through months of theory testing. Together, these leaders overcame potential project-killing problems and achieved a series of major breakthroughs that made the new technology ready for commercialization at INVISTA's Orange, Texas, plant in 2014. The process has performed beyond our expectations, once again demonstrating the importance of having A-level performers in leadership roles with focused responsibility for knowledge creation.

EXTERNAL NETWORKS

The result of the knowledge sharing sparked by an A performer moving from one part of Koch to another reminds me of the explorers from my grandfather's native country, the Netherlands. The seventeenth-century Dutch sent trading ships around the world, their routes stretching from Jakarta in the East Indies to Aruba in the West Indies—a span of more than 12,000 miles.

Innovations stimulated by the knowledge gained from this trade—such as better ship designs, windmills, and land reclamation—helped fuel a boom in the Dutch economy that transformed the lives of its citizens both economically and culturally. (Rembrandt and Vermeer thrived in this environment, which also provided refuge to revolutionary thinkers such as Descartes and Locke, and principled dissenters such as the Huguenots and Plymouth Colony pilgrims.)

The lesson is that societies are most prosperous when knowledge is most plentiful, accessible, relevant, and inexpensive. These conditions are best brought about by freedom of speech and association, and trade based on mutual gain. People make exchanges—commercial or otherwise—because they expect the transactions to improve their well-being. But even when exchanges prove unprofitable, they can provide valuable knowledge, as we tend to learn more from our failures than from our success. If we want to benefit from knowledge sharing in our organizations (which are essentially small societies), we must be open to more mutual exchange, as the Dutch were.

No matter how capable its employees may be, no company can match the world's rapid innovation and improvement with internal resources alone. To quickly apprehend relevant global developments, threats, and opportunities, a company must develop effective external networks to monitor ongoing changes in technology, methods, markets, politics, strategies, and people's values.

These networks can include trading partners, customers, suppliers, former industry employees, specialists, universities, technology developers, consultants, and other sources. Maintaining good relations and contact with them is essential for creating visions, strategies, and priorities, and for anticipating and understanding developments that affect business.

They also help identify, evaluate, and capture innovations, acquisitions, and projects capable of contributing superior value. Given the importance of MBM to our success, Koch relies on our networks to help us identify acquisition candidates with compatible cultures. The fit of acquisitions with our culture can be just as important as their fit with our capabilities, but finding that fit isn't always easy.

It has taken many years to build knowledge networks that have an understanding of our philosophy, capabilities, strategies, and fields of interest. The same is true for motivating those in our network to help us identify and capture the best opportunities. We pay our advisors based on the value they create for us, thus aligning their interests with ours.

Our networks have greatly expanded and diversified as we've added businesses and capabilities. For example, until the late 1990s, the biofuel business was unattractive to us because it was uneconomic without government subsidies. (Bad profit generated by political means is not the kind we're interested in.) But when crude oil prices rose and promising innovations in grain processing emerged, the equation changed. We realized ethanol could be a profitable business for us—even without the subsidies and mandates we opposed.

Traditional ethanol plants are woefully inefficient, converting only 33 percent of feedstock into higher-value products. Compare that to the 96 percent conversion rate of an efficient crude oil refinery. To evaluate whether or not the inefficiencies of ethanol plants could be significantly reduced, FHR developed another knowledge network that included inventors, animal feed consultants, and equipment suppliers. They convinced us such a transformation was possible, and they are now assisting us in the conversion of FHR's mills into more efficient biorefineries.

Among the improvements made or currently under way at FHR's ethanol plants are upgrades to the corn oil and protein, making them suitable for much higher-value uses. These improvements, combined with market conditions, led FHR to make multiple ethanol plant acquisitions. It is now the fifth largest ethanol producer in the United States, with an annual output of more than 820 million gallons.

As FHR acquired ethanol plants, it assisted Koch Supply and Trading in exploring ethanol trading and distribution opportunities. Networks are even more important for our trading-based businesses. By combining its exceptional worldwide knowledge sources and relationships with its superior analytical capabilities and FHR's asset base, KS&T (in partnership with Flint Hills) was able to build a successful ethanol trading business.

KS&T identified that opportunity by first understanding the industry's distribution problems, which were caused by fragmentation, reliance on railroads, pipeline difficulties, and risk-averse participants. Instead of just providing capital, KS&T viewed its role as an aggregator and risk absorber that could substantially improve the industry's efficiency.

It built relationships with transportation and distribution partners who could help it provide the best solutions based on advantaged access, scale, and optionality. A key to making this work was aligning incentives (see chapter 10) so all parties would benefit.

Once a network has been established, it is never exempt from the necessity of continuous improvement. We have found several resources and mechanisms that are beneficial for increasing the effectiveness of our networks.

One is to ensure that knowledge sharing follows the win-win principle. Leaders should ensure that their teams understand the value of knowledge and what portion of it should and shouldn't be shared with third parties. Proprietary trading insights and intellectual property—including trade secrets and details of business strategies—are all types of knowledge that should rarely or never be shared externally.

CONSULTANTS

"Hide and seek for $1,000 a week."

That was the mantra of a group of contractor employees working for us on a major turnaround at Pine Bend refinery in the 1980s. Their attitude was to collect their pay but do as little work as possible. (Today that would be "several thousand a week.") It was infuriating. And expensive. It came about because we didn't have adequate supervision to guide and oversee projects of that scale. The same kind of problem can arise when a company hires consultants.

Having worked for a consulting firm when I was fresh out of college, I know that consultants can be a tremendous resource for improving a company's knowledge about customers, competitors, benchmarks, disruptive technologies, trends, and public sector changes. If consultants' incentives are aligned so they're motivated to maximize benefit for you rather than maximize fees, the good ones can create significant value.

However, when used improperly, consultants cannot only

become an expensive habit, but leak proprietary information. To use them properly, a company must select only those with the right knowledge and values; define any and all assignments with sufficient specificity; have appropriate measures of progress; maintain rigorous oversight; and always ensure that incentives are aligned.

Large companies often develop an overreliance on consultants. This adds tremendous expense and undermines the development of the company's internal capabilities. One such company assigned its head of strategic planning the task of reducing consulting costs that were running $2 billion per year. As it turned out, consulting firms had burrowed into every part of the company, rendering it incapable of making decisions without them. The conclusion of every study was the need for yet another study. But when consulting costs were reduced by 75 percent in just one year, the company never missed a beat.

Likewise, when we acquired GP, it was spending tens of millions on consultants who developed good insights and delivered impressive reports, but those reports seldom resulted in effective action. We reduced GP's spending on consultants by more than 80 percent, replacing them with new employees (including a few of those same consultants who had the needed values, skills, and knowledge). This new arrangement provided proprietary and far more useful knowledge that actually led to profitable action at far less cost.

CONVERTING INFORMATION INTO RESULTS

Knowledge is information that is profitably used to improve results. Just gathering and sharing information that doesn't get results is unprofitable. Gaining information bears a cost in time and expense to both the provider and the receiver. Thus we need to ensure that we are not wasting time providing information that is nice to have, but doesn't improve results. (A major violation of this cautionary note is meetings, which need to be designed to ensure the value they create exceeds the opportunity cost of the participants.)

This is just as true for information technology, or IT, as it is for other information enablers. With that caveat, it is safe to say IT has played a critical role in our growth, enabling us to better gather and share knowledge, and to improve the utilization of our insights and capabilities. Each decade has brought ever-greater breakthroughs—from fax machines in the '70s, voice mail in the '80s, e-mail in the '90s, and search engines in the last decade, to the proliferation of the cloud and data-analysis tools we use today.

In our trading businesses, technology feeds real-time and historical data automatically to trading and variance tools, enabling traders to identify and respond quickly to changing market conditions.

In our plants, environmental and safety audit findings are immediately input into our online system, then directed to the appropriate personnel to enable proper follow-up and the identification of patterns.

In our human resource capability, recruiting has benefited from social networks such as LinkedIn and Facebook, and newer systems that are actually capable of finding candidates who haven't even applied for our open roles.

In business development, online private libraries catalogue extensive industry data and internal evaluations of projects and businesses, avoiding duplication of effort and memorializing important analysis and conclusions from past work.

Numerous applications of search and networking technologies have provided low-cost, rapid access to thousands of employees and third parties who help inform our point of view on opportunities.

Global engineering analysis and product life cycle systems extend the reach of collaboration with our engineering and manufacturing teams around the world, allowing true 24/7 product designs. Similarly, manufacturing execution and planning systems provide real-time views of our operations, enabling instant adjustments to schedules and faster reactions to customer and supplier changes.

The breadth, depth, and power of continuing advances in information technology are staggering. The combination of affordable and ubiquitous wireless communications, seemingly limitless storage, the increased computing power of handheld devices, and insights derived from the power to process massive data have led to innovations that have fundamentally transformed our business practices and the competitiveness of our businesses. When used properly, this technology enhances knowledge processes through the increased speed and lower cost of acquiring, storing, and distributing information.

For one, the adoption of open architecture by large platform providers such as SalesForce.com and SAP is spawning a revolution in new business process apps. This is enabling disruptive changes in our operating efficiency and sales and marketing effectiveness. To fully benefit from these innovations, our businesses are working to revise their visions to include more transformative use of information technology.

A prime example of this is GP's Commercial Tissue Business, which is using new communications technology to further improve its effectiveness in working with distributors and end users. Among the benefits are better coordination with distributor sales reps, improved ability to reach individual end users, and lower-cost sales calls.

At the same time, GP's Consumer Products Business is experimenting with direct consumer deliveries through e-commerce, which it believes can become a significant part of its sales. Both businesses are using digital media and advanced analytic tools—which lower the cost of distributing information and help turn it into knowledge—to create more value for their customers and end users.

Another transformative use of this new technology is a focus by all our businesses on the Internet of Things, which greatly increases connectivity—not only within the business and Koch, but across our global supply chains. In GP this includes experiments such as the "washroom of the future." All our businesses use the Internet to improve the safety and reliability of our manufacturing plants.

The ability of a business—any business—to transform itself through information technology requires several elements:

- Recognition by the business leaders that they, not the company's internal IT group, own the vision, strategy, and implementation for the transformation. IT organizations tend to promote systems that are state-of-the-art, but frequently not profitable. Business leaders too often don't have sufficient understanding of the technology to challenge unprofitable recommendations.
- Creating an IT organization with the ability to recommend technology that will be profitable in practice—in other words, people whose knowledge, values, and incentives are aligned with the entire business. The IT organization must also be capable in project management, technical and process architecture, data management, and security.
- Creating an innovation process that enables technology advances to be assessed and mastered quickly under guidance of the business.
- Restructuring and retraining the entire business organization as necessary to enable it to take full advantage of the new technology.

Perhaps unsurprisingly, the extensive use of information technology can result in cyberattacks. In 2011, GP's consumer tissue business was the target of a "denial-of-service" attack, in which criminals overload a company's website, forcing it to shut down and stop serving customers. Such attacks—many of them even more destructive—caused us to change our approach to IT security. We recognized that effectively dealing with this threat required expanding our knowledge.

As it turned out, the most valuable help came not from paid consultants, but from other organizations that had experienced similar attacks—a testament to the mutual benefit of knowledge sharing. The fact is, most companies by themselves can't keep up with the rapidly improving mix of tools and technologies used by hackers. We now share our insights with partners in industry, education, and nonprofits, and we gain valuable knowledge in return.

MEASURES

Knowing *why* something is profitable is often as valuable as knowing *what* is profitable. For this reason, a business must also develop measures that help it understand the drivers of profitability. Prices and profit and loss tell us what people value and the best methods and resources to satisfy those values. They are also the primary indicators of whether we are doing the right thing as a company.

In a true market economy, one in which prices are allowed to freely adjust, profit and loss is the market's objective measure of the value a business is contributing to society. To succeed, a business must not only develop profit and loss measures, but also determine their underlying drivers, in order to understand what is adding value, what is not, and why. This knowledge informs its vision and strategies, leads to innovations, creates opportunities to eliminate waste, and guides continuous improvement.

If it could be done, every company should measure the contribution of every employee, activity, and resource to the long-term value of the business and societal well-being. Unfortunately, this is impossible to do with any certainty or precision, since the long-term benefit of most activities is unmeasurable and the future is unknown. So we must settle for an indirect series of approximations, taking into account the opportunities, capabilities, and resources available to the firm, and the risks that are appropriate for it to take.

Remember our consultant in chapter 4 whose opportunity costs justified hiring an office manager and janitor? This illustrates why it is essential to rigorously examine all opportunities and alternatives. Waste is eliminated by prioritizing according to profitability, adjusted for risk and time. Working on a profitable activity is wasteful when there is an even more profitable activity that could be performed instead. But these calculations are impossible to make without knowledge of opportunity costs.

It sounds counterintuitive, but by considering opportunity costs, profit can actually be increased by *eliminating* some profitable, value-adding activities *if* doing so enables a business to capture higher-value opportunities. Even an asset that isn't directly part of a business should have both a P&L and a return-on-capital measure. This ensures that holding it is the best use for that capital.

We saw this after acquiring Georgia-Pacific. When GP was a public company, it owned a captive insurance company in Bermuda that required $275 million in cash to maintain. But after Koch acquired GP, its safety performance improved under MBM, lowering the return on that capital to low single digits (a good problem to have). There was a large reduction in the worker's compensation claims being insured, signaling GP was significantly better than other companies in its insurance pool. The opportunity cost of maintaining the insurance company became too high, so we discontinued it—a benefit of careful measurement and benchmarking.

But be careful: Measures are only beneficial if they lead to profitable action. It is tempting to measure things simply because they are easy to measure; instead, we need to measure things that matter, even when it is difficult to do so. "Not everything that counts can be counted, and not everything that can be counted counts,"[4] Einstein observed. The most valuable measures keep us on track in advancing our vision by enabling us to identify opportunities and problems, and by stimulating innovations.

In keeping with this concept, Koch's pension management group has developed measures that have significantly improved the profitability of our pension assets. These include the ability to monitor and forecast the risk in the portfolio on a daily basis. We target a specific risk level so that if market volatility increases due to a shock anywhere in the world, our positions can be reduced within twenty-four hours.

As a result, during the U.S. debt downgrade and potential default in 2011, we were able to quickly cut our investment positions by 30 percent, resulting in significant savings. Even though it is difficult to time the market in absolute terms, significant value can be created by understanding key drivers of variations in global equity performance and quickly adjusting the portfolio accordingly. In 2013, the return on our investments was more than double what it would have been if these adjustments hadn't been made.

A successful organization should measure—and do its best to understand—the profitability (and profitability drivers) of its assets, products, strategies, customers, agreements, and employees, and anything else for which it is practical to do so.

When we acquired INVISTA, it did not have profitability measures by plant or product. This made well-informed operating and capital decisions impossible and prevented the accurate determination of profitability by customer.

It also led to business leaders being overly focused on revenue, since that was one of the few measures they had. The result was an unprofitable proliferation of products. Leaders had no say in how overhead was allocated to product lines, leaving them without a genuine sense of ownership. Internal transfer prices were determined by formulas, rather than by a system that encouraged everyone to optimize for the company as a whole.

We immediately established profit measures and market-based transfer prices to create accountability for every line of INVISTA's income statement and balance sheet. These measures enabled leaders to see which businesses were doing poorly and needed restructuring (and why), and which were doing well and justified additional investment.

INVISTA has since developed an extensive array of other measures that have been big contributors to its progress. It now tracks all the factors affecting the price of its products and raw materials. This includes price-setting mechanisms such as supply/demand, trade flows, cost drivers, and the prices and cost structures of product substitutes. Besides leading to improved pricing, these measures have improved understanding of the attractiveness of internal infrastructure investments.

Leaders should strive to understand the rate of change in their industries and whether their companies or areas of responsibility are improving at a pace that is equal to, or faster than, competitors'. Changes in market share, rate of cost reduction, margins, and the percentage of profits from new products are all examples of such comparisons.

When measuring, accuracy should always be emphasized over precision. As we use the terms, accuracy is the degree of correctness that creates value. Precision goes beyond that, to near perfection. Perfection, thus, is the enemy of progress.

It is usually wasteful to develop detailed information beyond what is necessary to make good decisions. When evaluating an investment, unnecessary detail just distracts from the key drivers. Since it is impossible to predict outcomes precisely, trying to do so—as in making financial projections to several decimal places—is wasteful. Even worse, such attempts can create a false sense of confidence.

Given that we tend to work on what we measure, measuring the wrong things leads to waste and value destruction. An all too typical example is reducing *all* costs—not just wasteful or unprofitable ones. If your goal is to lose weight, you could accomplish it by cutting off your leg, but that is hardly beneficial.

Cost-cutting for its own sake is often just as shortsighted as overspending and can seriously damage future profitability. Many companies have undermined their highly profitable franchises by commoditizing them through cost-cutting. Various fast-food chains, for example, have commoditized their product by cheapening their ingredients. It is tempting to forget what the customer values and instead focus on the mirage of improving margins by using cheaper ingredients. A mud pie is certainly cheaper than chocolate pie, but it has no value for a hungry customer.

While measures should be quantitative wherever possible, qualitative and intangible components must also be considered, as they are critical to creative insights. Leaders should always ask, "What are the key drivers of value and cost?" and "How do we sustainably improve our competitive position?"

It is often a choice between offering products and services at a lower cost to customers, or offering ones of a higher value. At Koch, we have found that the cost-price-value model can help us measure the relative importance of cost-cutting versus customer value creation for any given product.

Michael Porter, the author of *Competitive Strategy*, observes that businesses try to gain an advantage by being either the low-cost producer or getting a price premium by differentiating their product.[5] The CPV Triangle helps us understand how to apply both of these approaches.

A cost-advantaged producer focuses on constantly eliminating waste. This is done by measuring and examining the profitability of every activity, process, person, resource, product, and asset, and by benchmarking.

If, after cutting costs, profitability drops when other factors have not changed, then we know that what was eliminated was not waste. Designing profitable cost-cutting initiatives combines marginal analysis with benchmarking, opportunity cost, critical analysis, and sound judgment. It involves determining whether something is worth doing because, as Peter Drucker taught, "there is surely nothing quite so useless as doing with great efficiency something that should not be done at all."[6]

Product differentiation can be achieved by understanding what

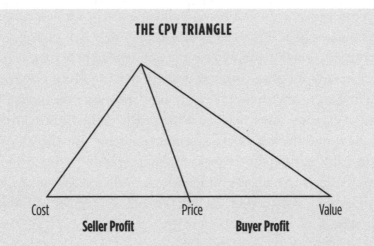

THE CPV TRIANGLE

Cost   Price   Value

Seller Profit   **Buyer Profit**

This simple diagram demonstrates how free exchange benefits both parties based on their expectations. The seller's expected profit is the difference between the price and the cost to provide a product, while the buyer's expected profit is the difference between price and the value to the buyer of that same product. Not only does price divide the total value between the seller and buyer; it determines whether there will be a transaction at all. A price below a potential producer's costs usually means no more units of the product will be provided by that producer. If the price is higher than the valuation of a potential buyer, then there will be no transaction and no value will be created for the buyer or the seller.

customers value now and anticipating what they will value in the future—another type of knowledge process. Based on that understanding, the producer must continually innovate to develop products and services that are more highly valued than those of either direct or indirect competitors. Creating more value for customers and capturing a share of that value create a better outcome for both buyers and sellers—good profit. (It is important to note that customers will value the product according to their subjective values.)

Businesses that differentiate their products are less constrained by competitors' actions. Price is no longer solely a lowest common denominator; it is largely determined by how much of a premium customers are willing to pay for the extra value provided.

Generally, a businessperson should attempt to be a price seeker rather than a price taker. This is best done by discovering new ways of creating value that are difficult to imitate. It is in both the supplier/innovator's and the customer's interest for the innovator to initially capture the majority of this superior value. This provides the incentive for the supplier to continue to innovate, since, given creative destruction, the portion he can capture will decline over time.

MARGINAL ANALYSIS

Marginal analysis asks, "What is the profitability of one more unit of production, of one more or less plant, or of a more expansive versus a more modest investment?" It entails weighing the costs and benefits of a change. We call it marginal not because it is unimportant, but because it is incremental, occurring at the margin. Marginal analysis looks at the benefits and costs associated with a specific change. This generally makes it a much more powerful tool than working with averages or totals.

Most decisions should be made using marginal analysis. This requires understanding the difference between costs and benefits that are marginal and those that are not, such as sunk costs. Only by making decisions on the appropriate margin will a business consistently enhance its profitability and eliminate waste. That margin will vary enormously depending on the decision.

To produce one more unit in a plant with excess capacity, the marginal cost would simply be the incremental cost incurred (which may vary significantly from the average cost), plus any effect on the market. However, if producing one more unit would require an expansion, the measure must also include the necessary investment and increases in operating costs.

Such increases are often underestimated, especially when the business has yet to experience the cost of handling the additional complexity and volume. In deciding what to do with an unprofitable plant, we use marginal analysis to compare the net present value of continuing to operate it with that of shutting it down or selling it. When used properly, marginal analysis is an indispensable measurement tool.

BENCHMARKING

Another type of measurement that can help eliminate waste is benchmarking—the process of identifying, understanding, and adopting superior practices from anywhere in the world. This can be done in several ways.

No matter what business we are in, we can all learn a great deal from the best in the company (internal), the best in the industry (competitive), and the best in any industry anywhere in the world (world-class). Analyzing such superior performance in a specific function—such as maintenance, sales, operations, IT, accounting, and so on—is a powerful way to learn what is best and how to achieve it.

In benchmarking GP's bathroom tissue business, we compared our costs not only to those of the other integrated majors, but to the most cost-efficient producers who specialize in just one segment, such as converting pulp into private label bathroom tissue. Best practices must be sought wherever they are, both inside and outside the company and even the industry.

Effective benchmarking requires objectivity, so it must be done with integrity. Such objectivity is sometimes painful, but it is essential to understanding the gap between our performance and the best—and what is necessary to eliminate the gap.

Although the information is harder to get, it is critical to benchmark not only against the largest competitors, but against those that are growing faster, are the most profitable, or have the lowest price. When we find they are better, we should never rationalize that it's because of factors we can't control. This self-protective thinking happens quite often and can be disastrous because it justifies inaction. Overcoming this tendency requires the humility to admit you haven't kept up, as well as having senior leaders who refuse to accept any excuse.

A measure that is generally not considered benchmarking but can bring many of the same benefits is comparing actual performance to the ideal. This is most readily done for physical processes using measures such as on-stream factors, yields, and energy consumption. The value gap between ideal and actual performance will indicate the priority that should be given to improving each.

It should be noted that nowhere in this measures section has the use of budgets been recommended. This is important: In general at Koch, we have found budgets to be ineffective as a management tool. In fact, they become absolutely counterproductive when they are allowed to create perverse incentives, such as basing bonuses on meeting a budget (which, in and of itself, seldom represents true value creation). Budgets can be very beneficial, however, when used as targets based on meaningful benchmarks, such as ideal or competitive performance.

PROFIT CENTER MEASURES

A business can best determine where and how to create value by developing measures around the concept of "profit centers"—any part of the business for which financial statements can be developed. Profit centers can be created wherever there are identifiable products, market prices, customers, suppliers, and assets. Their financial statements must reflect economic reality. Never forget that anywhere profit and loss is measured, analysis is also needed to understand what drives those results.

Identifying and efficiently creating profit center measures at the lowest practical level can provide a substantial competitive advantage. This includes knowing the profitability of every customer, which can't be done accurately when a business is allocating costs on averages, say by volume. Particular attention needs to be paid to low-volume customers. These tend to be high-cost when it comes to sales expense and where different product specs cause small plant runs or require additional inventory. Only objective analysis will determine the true cost to serve these customers.

Ideally, each plant—and each unit in that plant—should have measures that enable profitability to be calculated. If a plant makes more than one product, the profitability of each product should be tracked. When a business sells products or services to external customers, the prices reflect economic reality. When transferring products internally, prices should reflect the market alternative. As such, the internal price should represent the market price for the appropriate marginal volume. If the market is not liquid and there is a big difference in the price of buying and selling that volume, the transfer prices should be set between the two, usually at the average. There is no way to make sound business decisions without realistic transfer prices that enable profitability to be measured accurately.

Transferring products using a cost-based system leads to faulty profit signals and bad decisions. This is akin to the government subsidizing one business versus another, which distorts the market process and creates waste. Requiring business units to buy internally, when not done for good reason—such as protecting intellectual property or creating economies of scale—can be just as wasteful.

These profit-distorting practices are especially harmful when they are used to prop up a struggling business or plant. If an operation can't be made profitable—even when considering its effect on our other businesses—it should be sold or closed, not subsidized.

The purpose of internal markets is to provide internal signals, so that decisions are made on the basis of business profitability, just like external purchases. Proper internal markets generate knowledge, guide decisions, reinforce ownership and accountability, encourage entrepreneurship, and help eliminate waste.

Profit centers include not only the activities necessary to produce, sell, and deliver products to an outside customer, but also supporting activities, such as accounting and credit services. Given the difficulty in measuring the value support services are creating, without oversight they tend to maximize their services rather than their contribution to profitability. To minimize this problem, we put these services, wherever possible, under the relevant business or in an internal market.

Then we estimate their profitability by benchmarking and comparing it to the quality-adjusted cost of outsourcing. But it's not just the profitability of customers, products, and assets and support services that should be measured. As indicated in chapter 10, the profitability of each employee should be estimated as well.

This can be done by tracking, quantitatively where possible, the present value of their contributions (positive and negative) through the year and conducting annual 360-degree performance evaluations. The evaluations should include performance feedback from those who worked most closely with an individual during the year—ranging from supervisors and peers to subordinates.

CHALLENGE

Just as a country with free trade provides people with knowledge from all over, free speech within a company allows the exchange of information and ideas that generate innovation and progress. This free speech is a vital knowledge process. Diminishing or distorting communications within the business will inevitably affect the quantity and quality of its knowledge, leaving virtually everyone (except the competition) worse off.

Knowledge sharing isn't just important for innovation. Seeking, sharing, discussing, or challenging ideas and plans plays a crucial role in every aspect of an organization's success.

None of us has all the knowledge to consistently make the best decisions or discoveries. Because knowledge is dispersed and of various kinds, we need ways to ensure the relevant kinds are considered before making important decisions.

When a workplace culture of respect and trust is promoted, employees share their ideas and seek out the best knowledge to anticipate and solve problems. Verbal exchanges lead to the discovery of new and better ways to create value. When such exchanges are hampered by overbearing taboos, bureaucracy, systems, procedures, tenure, knowledge hoarding, egos, or hierarchy, knowledge sharing is stifled.

Leaders have to be aware that what they say or do often becomes lore and, when negative, can hinder the whole endeavor. Some of my negative reactions to losses cost us opportunities for many years. Because I was so critical of the large amount of money we lost in shipping in the 1970s, our people wouldn't consider opportunities in shipping for over a decade. I didn't make sufficiently clear that the error was not our involvement in shipping, but the way we went about it. This underscores the need to ensure that everyone understands what is being criticized, and what is not.

At Koch, truth is what gets results. It is what stands the tests of evidence and criticism—not what someone in the hierarchy declares is true. Continual questioning and brainstorming to find a better way is what we call challenging. It must be seen as an opportunity to learn and improve, not as a chance to kill another person's idea. Leaders should encourage challenges by asking open-ended questions such as "What are we missing here?" or "Is there a better way to do this?"

The quality of a challenge depends on having the courage and willingness to respectfully question anyone's—up to and including the CEO's—beliefs, ideas, proposals, and actions.

Challengers need to participate with intellectual honesty in the spirit of constructive improvement, rather than opposing something because it was "not invented here." They also need to make clear that they are challenging the idea, not the person.

Formal forms of challenges are called "challenge processes." One productive form of challenge process is a brainstorming session. It should include representatives of all the functions and capabilities that can contribute significant value to the discussion, such as business management, sales, operations, supply, technology, business development, and public sector. It may also be appropriate to include outsiders if they possess superior knowledge or a valuable perspective.

To be most effective, this kind of challenge process must include people with different perspectives, kinds of knowledge, and expertise. This is the kind of diversity that is important for innovation and reaching the best decision; it is also most meaningful and beneficial to the company, the employee, the customer, and society.

The quality of the design and leadership of such a formal challenge process is also critical to its effectiveness. The right participants in the right forum with the right leader working on a well-framed problem will lead to breakthroughs in solving formerly intractable problems.

An even more structured version of the challenge process is the compliance audit by internal or external legal or compliance specialists. Some people may resist these because they feel threatened or worry that they aren't trusted. Instead, the audit should be viewed as a chance to learn and improve. Would you rather find out you have a problem through an audit or by having a disaster?

To drive the process of creative destruction internally, nothing and no one can be immune to challenge. Each of us, from frontline supervisors to the CEO, must help foster an open environment that invites challenge and embraces change. If you find that your views are rarely challenged, it is likely that you are giving the impression that challenges are not welcome. Not only must leaders at every level be open to challenges; they must solicit them, and then thank any challenger who offers a constructive one.

Whatever the problem, it must be addressed lest it imperil the business. So no matter your role in the company, you should actively seek knowledge and alternative points of view. You must proactively share your knowledge and viewpoints with those who would benefit. When all participants in a challenge process embrace our MBM Guiding Principles and focus on creating value, the result is a powerful tool for discovery.

KNOWLEDGE AND VALUE CREATION

Thinking back to the knowledge processes involved in cancer research described at the beginning of this chapter, can you imagine the outcome for cancer patients if researchers' decisions were based on fear, defensiveness, ego, or perverse incentives?

Similarly bad outcomes await a business where decisions are based on destructive influences. Knowledge processes require economic and critical thinking, logic, and evidence in order to produce the desired outcome. Everyone should be explicit about the mental models they are applying and communicate them clearly. Avoid unnecessary complexity by keeping things, as Einstein advised, "as simple as possible, but not any simpler."[7] Elegantly articulated but complicated mental models, pointless arguments, and ideas that do not deliver profitable results have no value. Style should never take precedence over substance.

Free societies are exceptionally effective at communicating what people value and how best to satisfy those values. Likewise, within a company, a focus on the truth and ethical results using market-based knowledge processes can harness the power of free markets to produce useful knowledge.

There are always better, faster, and cheaper ways to create more value for a company, its customers, and society. Value creation requires good economic thinking, measuring profitability whenever practical, seeking and sharing knowledge, embracing challenges, and appropriately using proven tools and mental models. These are the essential elements of superior knowledge processes.

At Koch, we emphasize that the person with the best knowledge relevant to a particular decision should be the one to make it. While this is generally true, it is more accurate to say that the person with the comparative advantage should make the decision, which is the subject of the next chapter.

CHAPTER 9

Decision Rights

PROPERTY RIGHTS INSIDE THE ORGANIZATION

Men pay most attention to what is their own; they care less for what is common. . . . [They] are more prone to neglect their duty when they think that another is attending to it.

— ARISTOTLE[1]

THE TRAGEDY OF THE COMMONS

When I was a grad student in Cambridge I rented an apartment on Trowbridge Street with two roommates. This apartment didn't have a single right angle in it, and it was in a tough neighborhood. I once had to flee an attempted mugging while walking home alone at night.

Renters in the building were supposed to carry their trash down to the garbage cans in the alley via the fire escape on the side of the building. But lazy occupants dropped the bags off the fire escape instead, letting garbage pile up knee-high.

Even if an upstanding renter (ahem) wanted to dispose of his garbage properly, there was no way to walk through that alley, because of the trash pileup. None of us owned this alley or had the power to stop others from trashing it. So none of us took care of it. This is an example of what is called the "tragedy of the commons."

Ecologist Garrett Hardin coined that phrase to describe what happens when herdsmen graze animals on shared grazing land, referred to as the commons.[2] A rational herdsman will add as many animals as he can graze, because he receives all the proceeds when the additional animals are fed, and later sold, but he bears almost none of the cost of grazing—until the commons is depleted. He has no incentive to preserve the land for the long term, because he knows if he doesn't overgraze, someone else will. The point is that when no one owns or sufficiently benefits by conserving a resource, no one takes responsibility for it, and the resource tends to be used inefficiently, overused, or even extinguished.

Many of the things that go wrong or opportunities that go unrealized in business are a result of the tragedy of the commons— shared areas with unclear (or nonexistent) demarcation of responsibilities. At Koch, we use decision rights to replicate the benefits and responsibilities of property rights in society. Just as we think of employees as entrepreneurs at Koch, we think of decision rights as property rights in the organization.

A gut-wrenching real-life example of the tragedy of the commons was the 2010 Deepwater Horizon incident in the Gulf of Mexico, caused by a blowout and explosion in the Macando well that was drilled for British Petroleum by a rig owned and operated by Transocean. (Several Halliburton employees were providing technical support.)

Eleven rig workers died in the explosion, and dozens of others were injured. The resulting harm to marine life and environmental damage along the Gulf Coast was enormous.

When he faced the media that fateful day, BP's CEO seemed convinced where the fault lay. "The responsibility for safety on the drilling rig is with Transocean. It is their rig, their equipment, their people, their systems, their safety processes," he told CNN.[3]

But the explosion could have been avoided had decision rights been better established. Who among the three different organizations, and among all the people employed by them, bore responsibility and had the authority to stop unsafe procedures? Had BP realized the magnitude and probability of the risk it was taking when certain decisions were made, would the explosion have occurred?

As Aristotle's quote at the beginning of this chapter acknowledges, people tend to take better care of things they own. This is because the owners of a resource not only reap the benefits of its use, but bear the costs as well. When there is no ownership or it is unclear, the resource will be used wastefully.

Unless people have clearly defined areas of responsibility, it's difficult—if not impossible—to elicit beneficial proactive behavior, or to hold people accountable when things go wrong. When no one has clear ownership of a resource, no one can be held responsible for its efficient use.

In MBM, decision rights are synonymous with authority. If you have the decision rights to decide something, not only do you have the authority to decide it; you are responsible and accountable for it.

In a market economy, consumers ultimately direct an owner's use of property. They reward her if she serves them well and abandon her if she doesn't. Thus, if an owner satisfies customers, her property rights increase. If she doesn't, they diminish. Property rights are continually gained by those who use them most effectively to satisfy customers, and lost by those who don't.

The principle of decision rights is similar, though it is important to recognize that decision rights are more limiting than property rights. Since the company, rather than the employee, owns the property and the profits, the employee has a fiduciary responsibility to the company that should guide any decision rights. Think of them as property on contract. This is why our employees' decision rights are constrained by our Guiding Principles, including the obligation to create value for the company.

Similar to private property rights in society, decision rights in an organization can be subdivided and come in many and varied forms. Employees with broad decision rights over how their daily work is done may have much less authority over operating and capital expenditures or matters relating to other workers. At the same time, other employees' main responsibilities need to be ensuring that these expenditures are profitable and well controlled.

Decision rights should reflect an employee's demonstrated comparative advantages. As discussed in chapter 4, an employee's comparative advantages are evident in those activities for which she can create the greatest value compared to the opportunity cost of her time. When these are optimized among a group, the value it creates is maximized.

This concept is easily seen in salespeople. Even though they may also be very good at sales analysis, actually making the sale is a more valuable use of their time. So freeing top salespeople to focus on selling by utilizing technically qualified sales analysts to do analysis is an example of getting both focused on their comparative advantages. Employees who focus on their comparative advantages and consistently make good decisions will have expanding decision rights, regardless of their role or position in the organization.

Understanding and applying this concept—that the person with the comparative advantage to make that decision well (not necessarily the highest-ranking person) should be the decision maker—leads to greater value creation. This is often a hard lesson to accept for people with highly specialized expertise who are used to being in charge. Many doctors would do themselves (and their patients) a favor by creating a culture of knowledge sharing and letting nurses, therapists, and other caregivers exercise their comparative advantages more often.

Granting well-defined decision rights in this way flies in the face of hierarchical norms. Proper use of decision rights shines a spotlight on the inefficiency of organizations that emphasize tenure and pedigree over ability and results. Our approach to decision rights is one of the significant ways in which MBM sets us apart from other companies.

BRINGING DECISION RIGHTS TO GP

This dimension of MBM has been a major contributor to the improvement of companies Koch has acquired. A case in point is Georgia-Pacific.

Koch moved GP away from its old system of decision-making authorities based on pay grades and job titles, whereby items included in the "approved" budget required less authority than those that were not. Instead, we base authorities on a demonstrated comparative advantage in decision making, without consideration of the budget.

Like many companies, GP had a command-and-control structure in which challenge of leaders was discouraged. We broke down this strict hierarchy in which leadership seemed above and apart from the other employees. When we acquired the company, GP's senior management worked on the top floor of a fifty-one-story building in Atlanta, which had a special elevator. No employee was permitted on the floor without a jacket and tie—even though the rest of the company had a "business casual" dress code. Those who were periodically summoned to the fifty-first floor stored a jacket and tie in their office.

To dramatically reduce the impression that management was inaccessible and unimpeachable, Koch moved these leaders downstairs with their teams and converted the fifty-first floor into meeting rooms available to all employees. This was a symbolic but important change.

More substantively, we stressed that an essential part of everyone's job was challenging the boss if something was wrong or if she knew a better way. At Koch, leaders are required to encourage and welcome such challenges from employees.

Before Koch acquired GP, roles there were based largely on pedigree and seniority. But when Koch works with an employee to develop his role, responsibilities, and expectations, we look at the individual's comparative advantages instead. So we did away with overly detailed job descriptions and other unproductive measures. Responsibilities and expectations are now clearly and simply defined.

These last types of decision rights take some time to learn and apply, so we changed them gradually, over a number of months, accompanied by an extensive education program. Previous acquisitions had taught us that immediately redoing responsibilities and authorities often resulted in confusion and, in some cases, a halt or damaging delays in projects and initiatives.

We were able to change other types of decision rights more quickly, such as no longer using preordained budgets as an approval tool for capital expenditures and incentive compensation. Instead, the quality of people's decisions and the level of their authorities now determine these outcomes. As a general matter, budgets are not used as control tools—every decision is considered individually, on its own merits.

We then gave GP's credit department full authority on all credit decisions, a significant change from the way things had worked. Previously, although the credit department set limits, the business groups had the authority to override them without any concurrence. This disregard of the credit function, not surprisingly, had led to unprofitable credit decisions.

When the business units began partnering with the credit department, sharing their point of view and knowledge, the collaboration better aligned credit decisions with risk-adjusted profitability. Because most credit departments are punished for losses more than rewarded for net gains, they typically decline any applicants with a set threshold risk of defaulting. Koch encourages our credit analysts to take risks when the margins are high enough to justify them. The higher the profit margin of a particular product, the greater the credit risk we are willing to take.

Another improvement in credit performance at GP was rewarding team members based on how their decisions drove the profitability of the business, as opposed to based on simply whether credit losses were incurred or avoided. In an environment with clear decision rights, the owners of good decisions reap rewards, just as entrepreneurs in a free society do when they use their private property to create value for their customers and society.

OPTIMIZING DECISION RIGHTS

Koch's innovation rate accelerated as we applied the Decision Rights dimension of MBM across the company. Clearly defining decision rights and basing them on comparative advantage can similarly benefit any company of any size, in any industry or sector.

Competitively advantaged innovation requires working on the best opportunities, establishing a clear owner, having the right people in the right roles, effectively experimenting, rapidly and efficiently scaling up, and finding the balance between short- and longer-term disruptive innovations. In other words, the very nature of innovation requires a dynamic approach to decision rights, with frequent reviews and adjustments.

Principled entrepreneurs earn good profit—and with it, additional property—when they produce products or services that customers value more highly than their alternatives. When they fail to do so, they suffer losses, and their control of property diminishes.

This approach serves the socially beneficial function of constantly moving property into the hands of those who will better use it to help others improve their lives. "The market determines [who shall have what property and who shall do what work]. None of these decisions is made once and for all; they are revocable every day. The selective process never stops," wrote Ludwig von Mises.[4] Likewise, decision rights continually move authority to those who continue to use it to create good profit for the company.

PUSHING DECISION RIGHTS
DOWN OR UP

Proximity to a problem or process does not determine who is in the best position to make a decision. In a world characterized by knowledge-driven rapid change, top-down decision making is commonly criticized as being highly inefficient.

It is true that centralized command-and-control business management suffers from many of the same problems seen in centrally planned economies, where those with local knowledge are not allowed to solve the problem at hand. It is also true that the ideas and creative energy of all employees should be leveraged, but universally decentralized decision making has its own problems. Certain decisions made at the local level can be highly inappropriate when a broader perspective is required.

The rigid application of either approach—universally centralized or completely decentralized decision rights—is not the answer. Decisions about how to optimize daily operations in a refinery, for example, are generally best made by on-site employees. On the other hand, people farther removed, but with broader knowledge, may be better positioned to make a decision on what the most profitable product mix will be in five years (the time needed today to design, get government approval for, and build a new processing unit).

Decisions about commencing or settling litigation almost always need to be centralized. We have found that leaders of individual facilities or business units can seldom anticipate the second- or third-order consequences of litigation for Koch as a whole.

The same is true for IT platforms. When each plant selects its own systems, it becomes impossible to effectively optimize the overall business. The point is that decisions should not be made by those in closest proximity, but rather by those with the comparative advantage to make sound decisions, including the best knowledge.

The question of where decision rights should reside can be just as important as who the individual decision makers are. Although our business units have decision rights in areas of core capabilities, minimum performance standards are set by a small team at the corporate level. They provide overall guidance and support—especially in aspects that could create liabilities for Koch.

These groups include MBM, commercial excellence, operations excellence, human resources, legal, tax, public sector, accounting, treasury, information technology, and risk management. Of these, the groups that handle the largest potential liabilities are compliance and EH&S (as aspects of operations excellence), legal, tax, and public sector.

Setting performance standards at the corporate level is essential; otherwise a business might permit behavior that creates risks for our other businesses or Koch as a whole. To be clear, the corporate group doesn't tell the businesses how to comply with issues that directly affect them, but it does keep them from setting a standard lower than what is needed for Koch. This is how we make determinations regarding EH&S standards, the scope of commercial compliance, how the tax implications of projects are vetted, and how accounting systems and controls should work.

As discussed in the previous chapter, we use internal markets as a mechanism for optimizing decisions about support services. Koch Business Solutions is the internal organization that provides support services to Koch businesses that they don't undertake themselves, such as IT infrastructure, human resource transactional services, and facilities management. Businesses inside Koch are free to choose KBS or not.

It is worth asking the question: If you or your employees were allowed to accept or reject services such as these, provided by a different group in your own company, what would you do?

The fact that KBS's services are not mandated has been essential to its success. While one business may choose to use KBS's property tax services, other businesses are free to handle that function themselves. To justify its services, KBS must demonstrate to all its internal customers that it is competitive in both cost and quality. KBS's biggest advantage over external suppliers is its employees, who are aligned with KII's core values and have a strong incentive to create value for customers.

Changing circumstances can lead to a shift in where decisions should be made. One example is our recent decision regarding whether to own or lease rail cars. Of the more than 10,000 cars needed to move products in and out of our facilities, nearly 80 percent were usually leased. The realization that rating agencies were attributing these leases to us as high-cost debt, combined with our improved liquidity and lower interest rates, prompted us to reconsider ownership.

As a result, the leasing decision rights in each business—that is, the decision about whether to lease or buy—were moved to the finance department. Thanks to knowledge processes that take into account ongoing liabilities, our percentage of rail car leases has dropped to less than 30 percent, with a good return on the additional investment.

Another situation that prompted a change in decision rights was the increase in internal fraud following our rapid growth in the early 2000s. As we acquired companies and expanded our original ones, we experienced a big growth spurt—jumping from about 15,000 employees in 2004 to 80,000 two years later. By then we were no longer a small company with a shared culture and trust. We began to encounter unacceptable behavior from employees who were setting themselves up as vendors, stealing inventory, giving inappropriate rebates to customers, and taking kickbacks.

Our legacy businesses had no real tools for addressing this kind of risk in their respective companies—it hadn't been a big issue when Koch was smaller. The companies we acquired were using checklists and strict prescriptives carried over from the Sarbanes-Oxley Act of 2002, which had applied to many of them as public companies.

Faced with this disturbing trend, we had to do something. From our point of view, Sarbanes-Oxley rules tended toward form over substance. As is typical of so many government programs, the regulation was more about checking boxes than using the best knowledge, followed by an expensive external audit. This was the antithesis of MBM. Koch required a third way.

Our Decision Rights dimension of MBM provided the answer. We experimented by making it the responsibility of each business unit to determine what specific controls were needed to manage its risks, ensuring there were no violations of laws. Since each of our companies is unique, this enabled them to decide the right focus— rather than giving them some mandate from above.

In many (but not all) cases, decision rights were used effectively. In most businesses, we saw a steady decline in the level of fraud and abuse.

However, some of our businesses did not respond effectively. They either didn't address the risks appropriately or they pushed decision rights too far down, entrusting them to people without the required knowledge. In those businesses, we experienced an even higher level of fraud and had to pull some decision rights back to the corporate level.

Deciding where decision rights should be located is as important at the plant level as it is at the business level. As described here and in chapter 6, ownership-based work systems in our facilities have provided great benefits in both operating efficiencies and maintenance costs. In the typical operating structure, operations and maintenance have separate and sometimes conflicting decision rights.

In an ownership-based system, operators have primary ownership not only of the operating efficiency of their units, but of their long-term health as well. This motivates them to develop additional skills, such as routine maintenance, which improves productivity and reliability. The same is true for any role in any kind of business.

Initiatives developed by employees, if approved and successful, earn increased decision rights. Each employee must demonstrate the judgment, responsibility, initiative, economic and critical thinking skills, and sense of urgency necessary to generate the greatest contribution to the company, consistent with the company's risk philosophy. Doing this in a principled way is what it means to practice MBM's fourth Guiding Principle, Principled Entrepreneurship.

No matter the size or type of your business, widespread value creation throughout a company requires (1) that decision rights are continually earned, not granted or bestowed; and (2) that lack of authority is never considered an excuse for inaction—especially when the company is faced with a problem that needs to be corrected or an opportunity that should be pursued.

Everyone has the authority, and the obligation, to identify and take the initiative to address problems. All employees, no matter their position in the organization, need to raise awareness, propose solutions, and gain approval for the resources necessary to address any problem or opportunity.

Failing to take a critical action or share important knowledge—which happens most frequently in areas of joint responsibility—can have serious consequences, as the BP oil rig disaster showed.

Imagine the consequences if a required report to the government is not filed on time or properly completed because the business leader, operations supervisor, and compliance specialist all assume someone else is responsible. When in doubt, employees at every level of the organization should stop, think, and ask.

Those without the authority to make certain decisions should not be exempt from the need to exercise entrepreneurial initiative. The most successful entrepreneurs are those who are not deterred by a lack of authority to control resources. Instead, after identifying an opportunity, they persuade investors to fund their new ventures. If an entrepreneur can't convince an investor, he must try to reconfigure the venture into a winning form. If he can't, he is probably being saved from an ultimate failure.

Like an entrepreneur seeking capital, an employee without the requisite decision rights benefits from this same exercise. Employees who are granted decision rights prematurely miss out on the opportunity to learn from a rigorous vetting process.

As employees discover opportunities for innovations or improvements, they—like entrepreneurs—should be expected to seek out others who have the authority to act on those ideas and will benefit from the exercise.

DECISION MAKING FRAMEWORK

At Koch, we expect employees to judiciously use not only knowledge sharing, the challenge process, logic, and evidence, but also our Decision Making Framework to earn approval for their ideas.

We give employees several tools to help improve their decision making. Of these, the most important is our Decision Making Framework. This framework is designed to facilitate the best risk-adjusted decisions, whether large or small. It does so by encouraging use of the best knowledge to explore the full range of outcomes, identify ways to optimize risk, discover the best alternative, and prioritize the path forward.

The DMF includes eight elements (outlined below) that can be applied to decisions of all types. The appropriate time and effort expended on each element should vary based on the nature and complexity of the decision. And it's not essential to go through all eight steps. In some cases, not every step will add value. Only those steps that are necessary for making an intelligent decision should be used.

The eight steps in the Decision Making Framework are:

1. **Briefly describe the authority being requested.**
2. **Give the background and a summary of the value proposition.**
3. **Outline the objective with the strategic fit.**
4. **Prepare an economic summary with a base case, as well as other plausible scenarios that could make the project much better or worse.**
5. **Identify the key value drivers.**

6. Describe the key risks and mitigants.
7. List the alternatives considered and why the one shown is best.
8. Project the timeline for future steps.

Let's consider a simple, obvious decision—like replacing a $1 million heat exchanger needed to keep a plant running. If that decision is treated the same as a $1 billion acquisition, the framework is being misapplied. The decision-making process for a heat exchanger requires only steps 1 and 2 and needs no more than a one-paragraph justification for the funds requested and explanation of the benefits. Use no more steps or complexity than is necessary to make a sound decision.

Needless complexity not only wastes the time of those involved; it places unproductive obstacles in the way of profitable decisions, discouraging initiative and innovation. Slowing down the decision and making it more burdensome can cause opportunities to be lost.

Beware: Perfection is the enemy of progress. Time and resources should not be wasted seeking universal consensus or trying to anticipate and address every possible question. The amount of detail and the extent of analysis in a DMF should not extend beyond what is necessary for an informed decision. The focus should be on the key drivers and risks that could make a difference to the decision. The DMF's reviewers should be limited to those with the specific knowledge, perspective, and experience—and the *courage*—necessary to ensure that the assumptions and key drivers have been appropriately identified and challenged.

DECISION TRAPS

Effective application of the DMF (and all decision making in general) requires avoiding decision traps. These are predictable, sys-

tematic failings in judgment that afflict all human beings. Here are
some of the most frequent failings we have experienced:

- *Overconfidence* in our ability to make predictions and es-
  timates. By not considering a whole range of outcomes, we
  have made bad investments because we underestimated the
  downside, or we missed attractive opportunities because we
  underestimated the upside, such as dramatic moves (in either
  direction) in commodity prices. Another form of overconfidence is the belief that we can quickly make major improvements in an operation—particularly one in which we have
  little or no experience.
- *Framing* the question in a way that biases our thinking
  toward a faulty conclusion. A frequent cause of this is failing
  to optimize the base case to which the investment is being
  compared. We once invested $100 million to improve an IN-
  VISTA plant in Singapore that was losing $10 million a year.
  Sure enough, it improved; the plant began to net $5 million
  a year. But did we evaluate shutting down the plant instead
  of investing the $100 million in it? No, but we should have.
  In this situation, we behaved like many companies in failing
  to optimize the base case. (We wound up having to close this
  plant anyway, thus losing our $100 million investment.)
- *Anchoring* occurs when irrelevant information or first impressions have an undue influence on our decision. This includes the leader expressing a strong opinion early in the
  conversation. Preconceived notions, such as the assumption
  that natural gas can't go below $5 per mm BTUs, can cause
  us to miss the elephant in the room.
- The *status quo* trap biases decisions in favor of doing nothing different, fostering an unwillingness to change or innovate. IBM fell victim to this by wedding itself to mainframes
  instead of aggressively pursuing personal computers.
- Counting *sunk costs* encourages decisions based on past expenditures rather than future prospects, leading to decisions

that don't reflect economic reality. "Given all the time and money we've spent on this unsuccessful research project, we should try one more thing" is an example of sunk cost thinking.

■ *Information or confirmation bias* occurs when we preferentially look for evidence that supports what we want to believe, ignoring evidence to the contrary. This particular trap led to our disastrous acquisition of Purina Mills during our mid-1990s "gas to bread spread" effort, in which serious and inevitable losses from large hog-purchase contracts were ignored.

■ Being overly influenced by dramatic, memorable, or recent events, such as unsustainable margins, is called *recency bias*. It blinds us to future prospects and awareness of where we are in the long-term cycle. As one example, the drilling rigs we purchased in the 1980s, believing the oil boom would last, became worthless when crude oil prices collapsed.

■ *Confusing random events with patterns* leads us to believe we can predict future events that are actually unpredictable. An example would be assuming demand for natural gas will increase similarly every winter, ignoring the variability in weather.

■ Allowing a *leader's past rejections* to stop the consideration of good future opportunities. After we shut down our ship chartering business in the 1970s due to large losses, my harsh critique of our approach to that business had a chilling effect on employees' pursuit of future shipping opportunities.

■ The *conservatism* trap: When employees allow their personal risk aversion to get in the way of taking risks suitable for Koch Industries, they are not maximizing value.

As with all pitfalls, the first step in avoiding them is awareness. So first examine which have caused your organization the greatest problems in the past, and then make it a priority to examine all decisions to avoid falling into these traps in the future.

DIVISION OF LABOR

A fundamental factor leading to human well-being in societies is the division of labor and its counterpart, human cooperation. Specialization and exchange are much more effective at satisfying human needs than self-sufficient individuals working in isolation. The division of labor is responsible for the world's greatly increased standard of living, despite its huge population growth.

The power of the division of labor flows from our diversity as humans and the endless variety of nature, and it is made possible by private property and markets. The benefits of specialization and exchange come not only from learning curves and economies of scale, but from variations in skills, knowledge, culture, infrastructure, geography, natural resources, soil, and climate. If every person and part of the earth were equal in every way, there would be much less benefit from the division of labor.

But because no two people are alike in values, knowledge, skills, or circumstance, it follows that even employees who have similar roles in an organization should have different kinds and degrees of decision rights. We should also expect decision rights to change over time, as our businesses and our comparative advantages evolve and we make good or bad decisions.

Decision rights are a dynamic process meant to ensure that those best suited to do so are making the decisions. Too many businesses insist that decisions ought to be made by the highest-ranking person in the company hierarchy. But this should only be the case when that person is the one with the comparative advantage to make the decision. We have found that changing this mentality is especially difficult for companies that have developed an overwhelmingly top-down culture.

ROLES, RESPONSIBILITIES, AND EXPECTATIONS

NFL teams do a better job tailoring decision rights to individuals than many companies do (on the field, anyway). It starts when the coach designs game plans based on the specific capabilities of his players.

If he has a great pocket passer as quarterback, a good offensive line, and superior receivers, he will choose to pass most of the time. If he has great pass rushers, he will use a more aggressive defense. If he gets a new quarterback who is faster and more elusive, he will redesign the role to include more running options. If a guard is better at pass blocking than run blocking, he may be shifted to tackle on the quarterback's blind side. Since NFL lineups are in constant flux due to injuries, trades, and other factors, coaches must frequently re-evaluate individual roles.

But take careful note: *a role is not a job title*. It is a description of a position and its functions to be performed by an individual. Roles should be determined by the nature of the business, the organization's vision, its strategies, and the comparative advantages of the individuals responsible for executing those strategies. A role should be designed to fit employees' comparative advantages such that they can create the maximum value.

In many companies, a role is established by a traditional grouping of tasks to be filled by the person most closely suited for most of them. This generally results in, say, two-thirds of the role fitting a person's capabilities and one-third not.

If I worked for an opera company and were given the role of business manager, I might do pretty well. But if the tenor quit and I were given his role too, it would be a disaster since I can't carry a tune. Hundreds of hours of singing lessons and dozens of coaching sessions would make no difference, because I have very low musical intelligence. Such efforts would only demoralize me and perhaps make me bitter, and I might even be at risk of being hit by rotten tomatoes, not to mention the company's risk of going broke. Yet this is unfortunately the way roles are sometimes assigned—by trying to fit a square peg in a round hole.

A cookie-cutter approach to employee roles, responsibilities, and expectations is unacceptable because it ignores individual comparative advantages. RR&Es are quite different from traditional job descriptions, which tend to be generic summaries of tasks and duties. Instead, each employee's RR&Es should focus on maximizing value creation and reflect that individual's comparative advantages and opportunities.

Great care must be taken to ensure that each role is designed to truly fit each individual's capabilities. As Maslow explained, people perform best when their role is a challenge, but not so much so that they feel overwhelmed and defeated. Supervisors at all levels need to regularly ensure that each role fits the capabilities of the person occupying it.

If there is a need for a role that no present employee has the capability to fill—even after roles are redesigned—a new employee should be hired to fill it. But whenever someone leaves or a new person is brought in, roles should be re-optimized to match the new mix of comparative advantages.

Some of our worst problems have been created by leaders ignoring the concept of comparative advantage in filling roles. A few decades ago, when Koch owned only one refinery, almost all of its crude supply came from Canada. Our refining company's head of supply and transportation had three direct reports—one responsible for crude oil purchasing, one for gathering oil by truck, and one for gathering oil by pipeline.

All three were performing well, and the refinery was fully and efficiently supplied. But following a disagreement with them, the head of S&T had the purchasing managers and trucking leaders switch jobs, putting both in roles for which they were ill-suited.

The purchasing manager immediately quit, set up his own company, and began acquiring 20,000 barrels per day of the oil we had been purchasing. To get him to come back, we had to buy his company for $7 million. After such a fiasco, the head of S&T left Koch. Such are the consequences of ignoring the concept of comparative advantage. Today, such a situation would not be allowed to develop.

Koch uses RR&Es to define general areas of responsibility. Specific expectations accompany the responsibilities within a given role. Two people with similar RR&Es might, in fact, have different decision-making authorities. Authorities are decided independently of RR&Es, because one person may prove to be a better decision maker, or be better at different types of decisions.

Accountability occurs when a person bears the consequences (good or bad) of a decision or action. At Koch, the person making the decision and the person delegating are held accountable. This policy ensures that a culture of ownership, accountability, and appropriate delegation is developed to avoid inaction, abdication, or finger-pointing. For an organization to be effective, every initiative needs an owner with clear responsibility who is held accountable for its accomplishment.

RR&Es require an ongoing dialogue involving the employee, supervisor, and other interested parties. Each employee should be responsible for ensuring her RR&Es are current, accurate, and effective. Both employees and supervisors are responsible for ensuring that RR&Es focus employees on maximizing their contribution to advancing the vision of their business or group. Supervisors must give employees honest and frequent feedback and use performance reviews to help employees understand and improve their performance relative to expectations.

Because individual performances vary widely, so do levels of individual authorities. Decision rights tend to be lower with new, unproven employees, whether they are fresh graduates or veterans of an acquired company. Tenure, credentials, or titles are not reliable predictors of good decision-making ability. Demonstrated success in decision-making ability is what counts, and even then, only for that type of decision.

When done well, the process of defining and continually updating everyone's RR&Es and corresponding authorities creates enormous benefits for the business and its employees. Proper RR&Es establish clear priorities, individual ownership, responsibility, a sound basis for accountability, and scorecards for compensation based on results.

The process fosters awareness of changing comparative advantages among the many members of an organization. This process is also an essential step in connecting individual employees to the vision and strategies of their particular business. It focuses them on the activities that will most profitably achieve their capability's or business unit's goals.

Most important, it continually improves the company's ability to make sound, value-adding decisions. The process also encourages employees to use marginal analysis and opportunity cost to keep track of how they spend their time. As employees identify their most and least valuable activities, they can focus on the most profitable ones and get others with lower opportunity cost to perform less profitable tasks.

A role tends to have an associated bundle of responsibilities. These clearly define the products, services, assets, activities, and employees assigned to the person in that role. What needs to be accomplished with those responsibilities is articulated in the third piece of RR&Es: our expectations.

Expectations are written statements specifying the results required of an employee if the business is to achieve its objectives. Expectations should always be clear, specific, and, whenever possible, measurable. They should focus on the desired outcomes rather than on the activities that might be required to produce those outcomes.

Expectations must also be open-ended and challenging enough to expand an employee's vision of what can be contributed. This encourages experimentation and innovation.

A clear understanding between an employee and supervisor

(and anyone else affected) regarding priorities and expectations is critical. Expectations are most meaningful when they are measurable, even if the measures are subjective and approximate.

There is a temptation for expectations to be closed-ended (such as communicating that sixty-seven carloads must be filled every day), rather than open-ended (encouragement to maximize the number of carloads filled—to the extent that doing so is safe, compliant, and profitable).

The closed-ended form discourages innovation, while the open-ended form encourages the employee to think, engage, and innovate. The open-ended form leads to ever-increasing value creation by stimulating creativity. The next chapter, "Incentives," will demonstrate the importance of motivation in that regard.

CHAPTER 10

Incentives

MOTIVATING THE RIGHT BEHAVIOR

Ever more people today have the means to live, but no meaning to live for.

—Viktor Frankl[1]

Why, at the age of seventy-nine, do I put in nine-hour days at the office and then go back to work at home after I've exercised and had dinner with Liz? It's not for mortgages or tuitions (at least not anymore), since our children are grown, educated, and married.

I certainly don't claim to lead an ascetic life, but neither accumulating material goods nor amassing a big pile of money has ever been an incentive for me to work.

My motivation to work hard has always been my need to lead a life of meaning—a fulfilling life. I want to do my best to make a difference in the world. I would rather die for something than live for nothing. Making good profit—earned by economic means instead of political ones—is a measure that tells me people value my contribution. No wonder, then, that it is one of my incentives.

There are plenty of those who argue that many CEOs are paid too much. I agree, in the case of CEOs who owe their profits to corporate welfare. But why would anyone want to limit good profit when it benefits us all? If profit is generated by Principled Entrepreneurship—by creating long-term value by economic means—then the interests of the company are in harmony with the interests of its customers, suppliers, communities, employees, and society at large.

Every company should strive to leverage incentives to motivate all employees to fully develop and apply their capabilities to maximize long-term value for the company in a principled way. Just as MBM doesn't place arbitrary limits on employees' roles, responsibilities, and expectations, MBM eschews limits on what employees can earn. The only limit is the value an employee creates through Principled Entrepreneurship.

The fifth dimension of MBM focuses on how to align incentives in a beneficial way—not a counterproductive one. Just as there is a difference between good profit and bad profit, there are beneficial incentives and perverse incentives. When Koch employees create superior value for the company, we reward them in proportion to that value.

My father's stories about his experiences in the Soviet Union, told to me when I was a young boy, remain vivid today. Through those stories I grasped the importance of incentives early in my life—especially as I watched that nation deteriorate over the decades.

Ironically, even Vladimir Lenin—who claimed profit was theft—nonetheless resorted to incentives to achieve desired outcomes. After the Russian Revolution, Lenin forced peasants to sell their grain to the state at low, fixed prices. When the peasants began to balk, he dispatched the Red Army to seize their grain. This generated much resistance but very little grain.

Even Lenin could see coercion was not working. "Only agreement with the peasantry can save the socialist revolution in Russia," he told a 1921 Communist Party conference. Lenin then introduced his New Economic Policy, which allowed peasants to sell their grain at market prices—a policy that continued until Stalin's regime.

Societies with beneficial incentives—those that reward creating the most value in society—have tended to enjoy the greatest and most widespread well-being. Societies with perverse incentives have suffered from waste and corruption, and the vast majority of their citizens have languished in poverty.

In *The Tragedy of Liberation*, Frank Dikötter writes about Mao's efforts to control the rat population in 1950s China: "When people were given a quota of rat tails to be delivered to the authorities, they started breeding the rodents."[2]

Instead of replicating the beneficial entrepreneurial incentives of a free society, many companies rely on bureaucratic, one-size-fits-all point systems or pay grades, detailed formulas, profit sharing, and cost-of-living adjustments, despite the fact that these, like Mao's rat quota, usually motivate employees to do the wrong things.

For example, when a company rewards the role of manager more than the act of creating value, employees strive to become managers (and increase the number of people they manage), even when leading people isn't their strength. With our approach, when individual employees create more value than their leaders, they are compensated more than their leaders, no matter what their title. This is the same philosophy used by professional sports teams in which the top performers are paid more than the coach.

For leaders accustomed to hierarchical cultures, this can be an incredibly difficult pill to swallow. It also causes great discomfort for those who expect titles or tenure to determine compensation rather than results. In our experience, the same corporate cultures that struggle with our compensation philosophy usually have difficulty embracing challenge. Both concepts threaten their status quo.

Most employees in Koch want to make a positive contribution and do the best they can for themselves, the company, their customers, and society. As discussed in chapter 7, this is why we specifically screen and select based on a well-defined set of values and beliefs. Many companies have not established the necessary clarity on values and beliefs, and the rigor in selection, to effectively hire based on them.

Worse, many have incentives that actually reward employees who *undermine* long-term value. Among these are automatic raises (such as COLAs) and pay formulas based on titles, certificates, diplomas, seniority, or experience. These are not only bureaucratic; they are destructive to motivation and value creation. So are bonuses based on whether an entire group or company made its budget, rather than for value created by individuals. Only an exceptional person can resist such perverse incentives for long.

In companies Koch has acquired, budget-based compensation schemes led employees to such counterproductive actions as deferring profitable opportunities until the next budget cycle. Many of these systems reward positions rather than individuals and enforce rigid pay structures across similar positions. They combine such factors as the number of direct reports, training and education credentials, job complexity, and authority levels into a formula that produces a suggested compensation range for a given position.

This tends to discourage real value creation through innovation, discovery, and entrepreneurial behavior. Instead, it fosters empire building, an entitlement mind-set, bureaucratic or political behavior, and avoiding risks rather than capturing opportunities.

At Koch Industries, we do not reward roles or positions. We reward individuals for specific contributions and results, not for some generalized or averaged result. Communism has famously been summarized as a system that takes "from each according to his ability" and redistributes "to each according to his needs." MBM says, in contrast, "From each according to his ability, to each according to his contribution."

MOTIVATING SELF-ACTUALIZED PEOPLE

Psychologist Abraham Maslow taught, "All human beings prefer meaningful work to meaningless work."

"The problem for management," though, is "how to set up social conditions in any organization so that the goals of the individuals match with the goals of the organization." He continues: "This includes the need for meaningful work, for responsibility, for creativeness, for being fair and just, for doing what is worthwhile, and for preferring to do it well."[3]

Maslow defines self-actualization as the highest level of satisfaction and happiness that an individual can achieve. According to Maslow's theory, for people to become self-actualizing their most basic needs must first be satisfied: physiological (thirst and hunger), safety (security, stability, protection, order), belongingness and love (family, friends, acceptance), and esteem (self-respect and regard from others). Only when these are met can people fulfill their potential.

For those who are self-actualizing, work becomes part of how they define themselves. They need to feel they are working for a worthwhile cause or a good company and are benefiting others as well as themselves.

"Even if all these [basic] needs are satisfied, we may still often (if not always) expect that a new discontent and restlessness will soon develop, unless the individual is doing what he is fitted for," Maslow said.

"A musician must make music, an artist must paint, a poet must write, if he is to be ultimately happy. What a man *can* be, he *must* be. This need we may call self-actualization. . . . It refers to the desire for self-fulfillment, namely, to the tendency for him to become actualized in what he is potentially. This tendency might be phrased as the desire to become more and more what one is, to become everything one is capable of becoming."

Maslow's theory on the conditions for self-actualization has been very helpful to us as we have developed our approach to motivating employees. As Maslow defines the term, self-actualizing people are essential to the success of any organization, because they not only actualize their potential; they understand and accept their own nature, as well as that of others. They face reality, have positive emotional reactions, and are creative, self-governing problem solvers with good interpersonal relations.

MBM strives to create a spontaneous order of self-actualizing people by hiring, retaining, and motivating those who internalize and exemplify all ten Guiding Principles—those with integrity and humility who want to create real value. Toward this end, it's important for leaders to understand the potential and the subjective values of their employees. This is impossible without establishing open and honest communication in order to know employees well enough on a personal level to do so.

For some employees, nonfinancial incentives—such as being praised for a job well done—can be as important as financial incentives. But care must be taken to ensure that such praise is truly earned. As Maslow put it, "To be praised for what one does not deserve or to have one's accomplishment unduly exaggerated can actually be guilt-producing."[4]

False praise also tends to undermine respect and trust. This is a growing problem in society as a whole, especially when children have been conditioned to expect praise and rewards just for participating, rather than for the quality or outcome of their participation. I've never known dishonest feedback to be an effective incentive, though many a leader has been tempted to avoid a difficult conversation this way.

INCENTIVES AT KOCH

All incentives, whether financial or not, should motivate each employee to fully develop her aptitude to create value, to innovate and drive creative destruction. Even though optimum compensation can never be determined with precision, the value an employee has contributed should be determined as accurately as possible. A judgment can then be made as to the best form and amount of compensation.

At Koch, we use incentives to attempt to align the interests of each employee with the interests of the company, our customers, and society. Since we strive to profit by creating value for our customers and society, our philosophy is to pay employees a portion of the value they create for the company. We believe this approach helps us attract and retain the right people, and motivates them to be principled entrepreneurs.

By creating value "for the company," I mean the *whole* Koch company—not a particular group or business inside it, or on an individual's personal scorecard she's keeping in her head. If an NBA basketball team rewarded players solely according to the points they scored, an "every man for himself" mentality would result, and teamwork would deteriorate.

Rewarding a player for his overall contribution to the team as a whole is what is necessary to have beneficial, rather than perverse, incentives. This can be measured by comparing the team's performance when the player is on the court with results when he is not on the court.

All of the large acquisitions we have made came with incentive programs that were in conflict with MBM principles. These included highly structured, formulaic systems that based compensation on meeting budgets, provided insufficient differentiation, and displayed an unwillingness to meaningfully reduce incentive compensation when earnings or future prospects declined.

At GP, for example, incentives were tied to meeting the budget, even when a very low budgeted profit had been negotiated between business leaders and management. Pay was predominately determined by position and pay grades rather than by individual contribution. Incentive awards were capped regardless of the level of contribution and almost never zeroed out—even for poor performance.

GP's incentives, like those of all other Koch companies, are now based on individual contributions and business results. This has greatly enhanced the performance of GP employees and, thus, the performance of GP's businesses.

Bonuses are now paid on marginal contribution rather than title or tenure, with much greater differentiation (even for some employees under union agreements). All incentives fully consider the contribution to long-term value. Base compensation is now treated as an advance on the total payment for contribution rather than an entitlement.

Structuring incentives to bring about productive behavior without adverse unintended consequences is challenging. Incentives must not only signal what is valued most highly, but motivate employees to create value in a principled manner.

Again, what any individual employee values is highly subjective and combines both financial and nonfinancial components. Nonfinancial incentives include belief in what we are doing, challenge, competition, pride, recognition, satisfaction, enjoyment, helping others succeed, being part of a successful team, and personal development that leads to future opportunities.

Companies should strive to motivate their employees through incentives that are a mixture of financial and nonfinancial. Our Beaverhead Ranch in Montana is a good example. Most cowboys don't go into ranching just for the money. They value the lifestyle, of which a big part is working with their families. That's why we waived our nepotism policy at the ranch. We went even further and built houses on ranch property for each family. When we implemented these incentives, the ranch attracted a more capable and motivated workforce.

In MBM, the ideal incentives are those that best motivate each employee to maximize value for the company throughout his career. Where feasible, compensation should be tailored to each employee's subjective value, providing the highest value to the employee for a given cost to the company.

At Koch, our theory of compensation is not an easy-to-apply

formula. But its general thrust is determining an employee's contribution first by estimating how much Koch's value as a company has increased in a year—not only from that year's earnings, but from changes in its future prospects. If we could do so with any accuracy, we would then estimate how much the employee contributed to that increase in value, and pay her a portion of it (taking into account the difficulty of her contribution and the scarcity of the skills required for it). This would enable us to determine her total compensation, from which we would deduct base compensation, to calculate her incentive compensation.

Given Koch's size and complexity, it is impossible to accurately determine any of this. So we work hard to approximate it by using the following bite-size steps:

- We determine the value created by the employee's business unit, facility, or service group to Koch, considering current earnings and return on capital, change in capabilities, competitive position, and the risk-adjusted value of innovations and growth initiatives—that is, the prospect for future earnings.
- After thoroughly assessing all the employee's contributions to the value the unit created (positive and negative), we compare this to the contribution necessary for her base compensation. To the extent that her contribution exceeds this amount, we award a bonus or other incentive compensation based on that difference.
- Deductions are taken for any compliance or EH&S problems to which the employee has contributed. (If such problems are serious enough, they could wipe out the employee's entire award.) Additions to (or subtractions from) the employee's compensation will also be made if she has had a significant positive (or negative) effect on the unit's culture.

Incentive compensation is tailored to ensure that it is consistent with—and reinforces—the message we want to send the employee about her contributions and needed improvements. For this compensation to motivate her effectively, her supervisor must clearly communicate its rationale to her.

Directionally correct incentive compensation (it can never be perfect) is critical to making MBM work. When we veer significantly off, it sends the wrong message and is demoralizing. This is why leaders throughout the company make a considerable effort not only to get the numbers right, but to communicate the rationale effectively.

DISSATISFACTION AS MOTIVATION

Monetary rewards are powerful incentives, but many other factors are critical to creating incentives that improve societal well-being. Ludwig von Mises believed there are three requirements for humans to act: (1) dissatisfaction with the present state of affairs, (2) a vision of a better state, and (3) belief that we can reach that better state. When just one of these requirements is missing, people will not act.

Our application of this model led to a restructuring at many of GP's manufacturing facilities. The dissatisfaction came from realizing GP's margins were being squeezed because of the way it was managing and staffing its plants. Once we recognized that GP's practices were pushing it toward the fate of major U.S. steel and auto companies, we began to search for a better state by benchmarking the costs and practices of its most cost-effective (not necessarily largest) competitors. This enabled us to identify specific cost differences and their drivers. The path to a better state included changing plant organization and rethinking GP's hiring, staffing, and compensation practices.

By sharing the facts about our lack of competitiveness with employees, GP leaders were able to get many site workers to recognize the need for changes in staffing and pay structures.

If the goal is to develop a culture that will be competitive in the long term, it's crucial for a company to give its people the right amount of responsibility to seek a better state. If given too much, employees will fail and become demoralized. If not given enough, they won't have the challenges necessary to learn, develop, grow, and be energized. The business will then suffer from not having the full benefit of each employee's capabilities.

We expect leaders to provide mentoring and encourage challenges so that employees feel free to think and spontaneously use their ideas and knowledge to reach a better state. In our experience, an apprentice model is effective in developing employees. At Koch, this model entails four phases: I do, you watch; I do, you help; you do, I help; you do, I watch.

The application of all three requirements of Mises's human action model is essential to business. Companies that fail to provide these conditions create a culture of inaction (and a lot of white-tailed antelope). Companies that drive creative destruction through a culture of Principled Entrepreneurship do so by providing a vision of how to create value, facilitating timely decision making and appropriately rewarding employees.

ALIGNING INCENTIVES

Beneficial incentives motivate most people to work harder, be more creative, and produce more value for others. In doing so, they benefit themselves.

These are not, however, the only reasons for using incentives. Even when well-intentioned and motivated people are eager to succeed, they still face the challenge of understanding where and how to focus their time and effort. Successful entrepreneurs use the incentives of the market to determine the most productive course of action. Likewise, employers should use incentives to guide employees toward areas where their capabilities, attention, and effort can create the most value, while enabling them to be more self-actualizing.

A successful system of incentives must align the individual interests of employees with the general interests of the company. If a result will be good for the employee, it must also be good for the company. Conversely, if the result will be bad for the company, it must also be bad for the employee.

This is especially true in all areas of compliance. To conduct business otherwise invites disaster. The effectiveness of our compliance program increased dramatically once we began to hold everyone (especially those in the management chain) responsible for an area in which a compliance problem occurs—and adjusted their compensation accordingly.

A number of years ago, even after I had been preaching the importance of compliance in talk after talk, the manager of one of our smaller facilities decided it wasn't necessary to do the required testing on asphalt we were supplying to a state government. (He had decades of experience with this specific job, but sometimes longtime experience can be more dangerous than inexperience—if it leads to complacency and hubris.) When we found out, we terminated the manager, disclosed the problem to the state, and came up with more effective ways to monitor compliance.

Still, what this experience told me was that my extensive efforts to convince others of the importance of compliance had fallen short. That deeply troubled me. So I called in the leader of that group to determine how this had happened and how it could be prevented in the future. This leader contended he couldn't have prevented it since he didn't even know the manager in question. I asked, "If we can't hold you accountable, who can we? You control and are responsible for who is hired and fired, and the systems and culture of your group."

Following that exchange we made clear, by cutting—or eliminating—leaders' bonuses according to their degree of responsibility, that all of them were fully responsible for any compliance, safety, or environmental problem in their organization, and that any such event would—at the very least—result in a major reduction in their incentive compensation. The amount of reduction would depend on the actual and potential severity of the problem.

Once our leaders realized their compensation could be dramatically reduced or their role changed, they quickly became much more focused on compliance and EH&S, and our performance improved markedly. If we don't hold employees (especially leaders) accountable for results and instead continue to compensate them the same regardless of their performance, we undermine the whole system.

Whether the objective is improving compliance, increasing return on capital, or anything else, the first goal of incentives, then, is to harmonize the interests of the individual with those of the company. This reinforces our individual employee's desire to do the right thing and help the company prosper.

Second, compensation should be consistent with the notion that no two employees are alike; thus, their compensation can vary considerably depending on the value of their contributions. As a result of differences in vision, desire, values, and ability, people vary in the advantage they take of the nearly limitless opportunities to create value. This is why two employees performing similar roles may well be compensated differently.

Third, no limit should be put on an employee's compensation, so employees will not put a limit on the value they create. Finally, incentives should be structured in such a way that the company can effectively attract, motivate, and retain principled entrepreneurs.

These goals are accomplished by rewarding contributions to the long-term value of the company, which include not only contributing to current earnings, but capturing opportunities that aren't immediately profitable, like multiyear research projects, building capabilities, and improving our culture. Likewise, refusing to reward activities that do not produce results creates a process that beneficially guides behavior and motivates individuals to do the right thing.

To align interests, overall compensation must be higher when margins and general profits are better and lower when they are not. Generally speaking, if this year's profits increase 20 percent (without any deterioration in future prospects) and an employee's contribution is the same as last year's, we would increase that employee's incentive compensation by roughly 20 percent. If his contribution were more or less than the prior year's, his compensation would vary from this amount accordingly.

Whatever the level, compensation needs to reflect the contributions of each person. Even if a business has no current earnings, some incentive compensation should be paid to those few who significantly reduce the loss or improve prospects for the future. If a business were going to lose $10 million but someone finds a way to reduce that loss to $6 million, she would be rewarded for saving that $4 million.

Effective leaders think about value creation broadly. They realize that employees create value not only by innovating or capturing a single opportunity, but by helping keep the whole value creation process (the business) running smoothly.

For instance, providing useful financial information to guide business decisions in a timely and cost-effective manner can be just as important to long-term profitability as keeping a plant running properly. That capability should be appropriately recognized and rewarded.

INCENTIVES AND FAILURE

After nearly 10,000 failed experiments in developing a new battery, Thomas Edison was once asked, "Isn't it a shame—you haven't been able to get any results?"

"I've gotten a lot of results!" he replied. "I know several thousand things that won't work!"[5]

Confusing as it might seem, failure and getting results are not mutually exclusive. When driving experimental discovery within a company, failure is not desirable, but should be expected. Sometimes today's positive results can only be derived from the lessons of yesterday's failed experiments. As Einstein observed, "Failure is success in progress."[6]

To be clear, I'm not suggesting that an organization reward failure. Although we should expect it on occasion, we should nevertheless strive to avoid it. And in addition to learning from our failures, we must learn from the *type* of failure. We need to recognize whether a failure resulted from poorly thought-out or impulsive action, or whether it belongs to that percentage of failures to be expected from prudent risk-taking, such as well-designed experiments or bets.

These different types of failures should be treated very differently when a company is designing incentives. By not unduly penalizing well-planned experiments that fail, we fuel an engine of small and frequent bets that can generate powerful discovery and learning. This is vital to innovation, growth, and long-term profitability.

When encouraging appropriate experimentation, we must recognize that benefits seldom come immediately. Accordingly, incentives must be designed to reward progress toward ultimate commercialization—as well as the valuable knowledge created for other parts of Koch.

The basic philosophy should be to pay for value as it is created, and progress toward commercialization creates value. Companies, such as Enron, that paid bonuses on the projected profits from a deal as soon as it was made (rather than when profits were realized) promoted disastrous behavior. Enron employees scrambled to make dubious deals simply because they could project a large profit. In contrast, at Koch we only pay a modest amount at the consummation of a deal, as an advance based on its apparent attractiveness. Further compensation is paid as value is realized. This includes rewarding those who have since moved to other roles.

It is particularly difficult (but very important) to align incentives across organizational boundaries. At Koch, this can involve transactions within a Koch company or across companies, such as transfers from fuels to chemicals at the Corpus Christi refinery, or a crude oil sale from Koch Supply & Trading to Flint Hills Resources. Transfers should be done in a way that helps us maximize long-term value for Koch Industries as a whole, not just for a particular business unit. Factors include the market price for a particular quality and volume, and the opportunity cost for both the buyer and seller. Compensation for employees engaged in such transactions is adjusted according to how well they maximize that overall value.

MARGINAL CONTRIBUTION

To achieve good profit, companies should pay people in a way that motivates them to create maximum long-term value, while faithfully following our Guiding Principles. One of the best ways to do this is to pay them a portion of the value they create for the firm, the way an entrepreneur receives a portion of the value he creates in society. Total compensation should reflect total contribution.

Assessing the total contribution (value creation) of an employee forms the foundation for incentive decisions. A leader must ask: What specific results or value are attributable to the actions or decisions of the employee? Did the employee initiate the idea or action? Has the value been realized by the business? What effect did this individual have on the value creation of others? Was the employee's contribution to the culture positive or negative?

Additional insight into an employee's contribution may be derived by applying the tool of marginal analysis. Being able to estimate an employee's marginal contribution—that is, the portion of value created that can be assigned to a specific change, factor, or individual—is an important element in an effective compensation system.

Koch's Talent Planning process (see chapter 7), which uses marginal analysis, calls for retaining employees who contribute at or above the median of all their peers doing similar work (especially at our primary competitors). We might refer to this median contributor as a typical contributor.

With the base case defined, an employee's marginal contribution is estimated as the contribution above or below that expected of a typical contributor. Employees who create more value than the typical contributor create a competitive advantage for the business and produce a marginal contribution. Employees who are contributing less put the business at a competitive disadvantage and may even be seen as producing a negative marginal contribution. If there are enough of these employees in a company, it will go out of business.

Leaders should track employee performance throughout the year, not just at year-end. We use economic analysis and 360-degree feedback (meaning an employee is assessed by those who have worked most closely with him, not just his immediate supervisor) to understand an individual's contribution to long-term results.

Employees are also asked to complete a self-assessment highlighting what they believe to be their marginal contributions. This is to ensure that the best information available is used to appropriately recognize both positive and negative contributions. The evaluation should include past contributions that haven't been fully compensated, such as a contribution to an acquisition in a previous year that is just now paying off. Positive and negative carryovers such as these often result from projects put in motion long ago.

At Koch, base pay is recognized as an advance payment for the value an employee is expected to create for the company. So what happens when an employee adds more value than was originally reflected in that base pay? The employee shares in that extra value, just like an entrepreneur in the marketplace.

There are several tools for accomplishing this, including base-pay adjustments, annual incentive compensation, spot bonuses, deferred compensation, and other incentives. A key role of managers is to retain and motivate employees who are adding superior value. By paying for value created, we help ensure the firm's competitiveness.

Even profit-making employees have room for further improvement. I don't consider any work I do "good enough"—because complacency and eventual decline are embedded in that mental model. No matter how high an employee's marginal contribution, his supervisor should still communicate how both the company and the employee would benefit from increased value creation. Employees who embrace and internalize this feedback will increase their marginal contribution and, thus, their compensation.

Conversely, unprofitable employees—those who create less value than their compensation and other costs (or even less than the median of their peers at competitors)—are wasting the organization's resources and destroying value. Unless their performance improves or a role is identified for which they can provide sufficient value, they must exit the company.

We recognize our incentive system is more demanding to administer than budget-, formula-, or hierarchy-based systems. However, in our experience, the effort Koch expends connecting employees to how they can create more value—and rewarding them for it—causes them to greatly increase their contribution.

PERVERSE INCENTIVES

Many common bonus plans create perverse incentives. These include homogenized profit-sharing plans, and bonuses that are a fixed or modestly varying percentage of base pay (regardless of contribution)—if the business meets certain financial targets.

One problem with these approaches is that since top performers get little or no more than poor performers, they have little incentive to make a bigger contribution. (In free societies, entrepreneurs who create more value receive more reward—and that is a major motivating factor. MBM recognizes this.)

Another problem is that employees will sacrifice activities that lead to long-term value creation to meet these short-term targets, such as not pursuing an opportunity that won't be profitable for several years.

Some companies institute fixed budgets as a way of controlling costs. Under this system, profitable opportunities are often missed as managers reject profitable proposals that would exceed their budgets. It is also common for a company to attempt to reduce costs by ordering an across-the-board 10 percent reduction in budgets or staff. This practice usually results in removing profitable expenditures and people along with unprofitable ones, leaving the company less profitable overall. Both of these errors create perverse incentives.

Perverse incentives are all too common in company/employee relationships. One of the most frequent is known as a principal/agent problem. This problem tends to be created whenever a principal (owner) hires an agent (consultant, broker, or employee). The principal desires the agent to act in the best interest of the principal, while the agent typically wants what is best for herself.

These conflicting interests manifest themselves in various ways. In cases where the principal and the agent have different risk profiles, the problem typically takes one of two forms. In the first, agents are extremely risk averse, generally due to lack of reward for profitable risk-taking and excessive penalties for losses from prudent risk-taking. The result is a play-it-safe culture.

Remember the question we looked at in chapter 7: Should an employee work on an investment with a 90 percent chance of making $100,000 rather than one with a 50 percent chance of making $1 million? As in that case, riskier opportunities are often in a company's interest, so a company's incentive structure needs to encourage prudent risk-taking.

To discourage excessive risk aversion, we reward total value creation and only make an extra deduction from incentive compensation for a loss when it was poorly thought-out or poorly managed. Also, the profits forgone from a missed opportunity are considered similar to losses from a failed venture—but to a lesser extent.

The value of missed opportunities and other shortcomings should be estimated and included when determining an employee's compensation (and communicated to the employee along with his compensation). During the 1990s, a risk aversion toward making acquisitions developed, and some leaders passed on opportunities to acquire high-quality assets. The opportunity cost of those missed opportunities was calculated and included in their evaluations—which quickly changed their behavior.

Similarly, consideration of opportunity cost helps eliminate waste and delay in our project approval process. When participants in the approval process seek to understand and mitigate risk beyond the point of diminishing returns, excess steps and analysis slow things down. This can jeopardize opportunities by making it impossible to get approvals quickly and efficiently. Factoring in missed opportunities better aligns the interests of those involved in the approval process with those of the company.

Consider, on the other hand, the employee who takes imprudent or even unauthorized risks—another kind of agency problem. These individuals hope to make a great deal of money for themselves by going for broke, even if it puts the company at risk. Such rogue employees, operating out of personal interest at the expense of the general interest, have destroyed entire companies—as we have seen again and again throughout history.

This destructive behavior can be minimized by selecting and retaining employees, foremost, on values and beliefs (see chapter 7), then appropriately setting decision rights with effective controls (see chapter 9), and aligning the success of the employee with the long-term success of the company.

Another type of perverse incentive is endemic at publicly traded companies: the quarterly earnings report. Management at a public company is under a great deal of pressure to meet quarterly earnings forecasts, because falling slightly short can cause a significant drop in the stock price. Consequently, management is motivated to make decisions that optimize short-term earnings at the expense of maximizing real long-term value.

Such decisions may include underinvesting in attractive cyclical or long-term opportunities, ignoring needed write-downs, or even manipulating the books. Perverse incentives like these make managing a public company extremely difficult. They also make it clear why Koch Industries prizes its private status, and why I'd counsel any entrepreneur to do everything possible to keep her company private, no matter how big it grows.

ALIGNING INCENTIVES EXTERNALLY

While this chapter focuses on incentives for employees, incentives are also important in aligning the interests of a company's other constituents, such as customers, suppliers, contractors, shareholders, distributors, agents, communities, and governments. By properly aligning the incentives of all these constituents through an understanding of their subjective values we greatly improve our ability to succeed.

Imagine, for example, you want to encourage retailers to preferentially promote your products. By understanding their incentives and subjective values, you can motivate them to recommend your products and provide premium shelf space by demonstrating that doing so will improve their store traffic.

Motivating external parties to support the company also requires that our employees deal with them in a way that is in the best interest of the company as a whole. If even one of our businesses develops a bad relationship with a supplier, customer, government agency, or other constituent, it will probably hurt other parts of Koch.

We have found that aligning incentives with performance almost always improves outcomes. This is why we attempt to align incentives with our external advisors—as well as our employees, though it isn't always easy. Investment bankers, real estate brokers, and other advisors often claim they bring comparative advantage to a project, but most hesitate to accept a compensation structure based on performance. Their position is typically that incentives are already aligned because if a client does not complete the transaction, no payment is due. We don't accept this argument.

In our view, for an adviser to be beneficial, he must achieve a better value than we could have achieved on our own. Thus we want a compensation arrangement in which the advisor shares in that gain. And as a seller, when a transaction is at a lower value than expected, we want that payment to be lower than the typical market rate. We incorporate this framework into our advisor contracts, whether buying or selling.

In one transaction, we were convinced we had identified the only possible buyers for a small business owned by Koch Chemical Technology Group. But when a banker convinced us that he could add value by expanding the potential buyer pool, we agreed that his compensation would be adjusted up or down depending on whether this proved to be true. It turned out to be true, with a result far superior to what we could have achieved on our own. The entrepreneurial banker was compensated accordingly.

Bankers typically seek a fee ranging from 1 to 2 percent of a transaction, depending on its size. Consider an example in which the banker would charge 1 percent for selling a business that we value at $100 million, and which she feels confident she can sell for our $100 million "hold value." If the ultimate sales price is $120 million, the banker will receive $1.2 million.

Although this is better than $1 million, most advisers would not risk a failed transaction—even if the probabilities are relatively low—by seeking the highest valuation in the market. She would only earn $200,000 more if she sold the business for $120 million, but the risk of the deal collapsing at that price might rise to 30 percent.

So to reward her risk-taking, we might offer a 5 percent commission on the first $10 million above the $100 million, and a 10 percent commission on the next $10 million. In this scenario, the 30 percent chance of failure is mitigated by the opportunity to earn $2.5 million in commission, rather than just $1.2 million. The incentives are then aligned because we have a 70 percent chance of increasing our value by $20 million, less commissions.

It is just as critical for a business to align incentives with the communities in which it operates. At Koch, we attempt to do this by understanding what they value. Most communities want good neighbors who strive to make the community a better place by operating safely, protecting the environment, and providing good jobs. This is why we expect our employees to not only achieve EH&S excellence, but to be good citizens who contribute to the community, and why the company also supports local charities that are consistent with our values.

We use the same approach with all levels of government that have authority over our operations. In our dealings with government representatives, we do our utmost to act with the highest integrity and to always perform on our promises. When we have a problem or make a mistake, we take responsibility by quickly acknowledging and correcting the situation, and then trying to prevent it from reoccurring.

We do this not only because it's the right thing to do, but because communities and governments are more likely to allow companies to grow and prosper when those firms act with integrity and are environmental, safety, and compliance leaders. Everyone, except poorer-performing competitors, benefits when new and better jobs are created by Principled Entrepreneurship.

Beneficial incentive systems do more than align our interests and signal what is valued. They help employees understand true value creation. To do meaningful work is to contribute—to generate good profit by creating value in society. Beneficial incentives encourage all of us not only to lead productive lives, but to realize our full potential and find satisfaction and fulfillment in our work—which is, indeed, my incentive for working hard.

PART III

CHAPTER 11

Spontaneous Order in Action

FOUR CASE STUDIES IN
MARKET-BASED MANAGEMENT

Spontaneous order provides "a more efficient allocation of societal resources than any design could achieve."

—F. A. Hayek[1]

"And finally, monsieur, a wafer-thin mint."

Any Monty Python fan will remember this John Cleese line from *The Meaning of Life*, in which Cleese, as a slick restaurant maître d', pushes one last course on a grotesquely over-fed diner who finally explodes.

Monty Python films are often brilliant expositions of the disastrous consequences when people don't use reality-based mental models to guide their actions. As noted in chapter 3, any business with behavior based on faulty mental models will eventually fail. Just because we—like the diner who thought he could ingest one more morsel—believe or want a thing to be true does not make it so. "Everyone is entitled to his own opinions, but not his own facts," the late Senator Daniel Patrick Moynihan quipped.[2]

Another classically absurd Monty Python scene that speaks to this tendency is the witch trial in *Monty Python and the Holy Grail*, in which a dim-witted knight-to-be imparts medieval logic to a crowd of townspeople hell-bent on finding a witch to burn.

Witches burn because they are wood, he reasons. Another property of wood is that it floats on water. What else floats? Ducks. Therefore, he concludes triumphantly, if she weighs the same as a duck, she's a witch, and the townspeople are permitted to burn her.

It doesn't take a comic genius to lay bare the consequences of not using a reality-based framework for problem-solving. But it helps.

As we have seen, MBM is a reality-based tool that enables every employee to innovate and solve problems without being told precisely how. Its goal is to create a spontaneous order by providing employees with a simplified set of principles and reality-based mental models to guide their actions and decisions. The models are then organized into a toolkit to make them usable as a problem-solving process. In the preceding chapters, I have laid out the individual tools. Think of this chapter as the toolkit.

THE MBM FRAMEWORK AND PROBLEM-SOLVING PROCESS

Einstein saw the divine in the "orderly harmony of what exists."[3] If one thinks of the natural world as functioning harmoniously without orchestration or central planning, one can easily visualize spontaneous order—an order that leads to the miracles of nature. The intention of MBM is to set the conditions of an organization—a framework consisting of a structure, a way of thinking, and a culture—to bring about a spontaneous order that produces its own miracles.

An organization can create this order when its members are dedicated to a sound vision and the right people are in the right roles with the right values, knowledge, authorities, and incentives.

The application of the five dimensions of the MBM framework to bring about such spontaneous order is one of our most important innovations at Koch. As with all innovations, it was developed and refined over time through experimental discovery.

When used to solve a problem, the five dimensions enable us

to more readily identify its causes and cures. When applied as a lens to envision a new model for a business, the application of the framework can be transformative. Since its evolution began in the 1960s, we have discovered that case studies are the best way to illustrate how to get results from MBM. Following are four real-life cases from within Koch. In each example, the application of all five dimensions is illustrated.

Please note that these cases illustrate how the MBM framework can work for any type of business, business function, or kind of problem.

Case Study #1:
Georgia-Pacific Consumer Products

In 2005, Koch made its biggest acquisition in company history. To acquire Georgia-Pacific, we took it deep into debt—to the point that unless performance improved, Georgia-Pacific would be in violation of its loan covenants (commitments to the lenders concerning the company's financial condition) that tightened over time.

Back then, Consumer Products—Georgia-Pacific's largest division, with almost 40 percent of its business—was struggling. Some of its brands were losing market share and in danger of being dropped by major customers. In 2007, Consumer Products was ranked last by its customers as a strategic partner when compared to its largest competitors. Georgia-Pacific's stated strategy of being a "fast follower"—not investing in research, but instead imitating successful products and selling them at a lower price—wasn't allowing it to stay competitive.

We acquired Georgia-Pacific because we believed MBM and our related core capabilities could create value in its businesses. Our acquisition of its pulp business the year prior had not only validated that assumption, but convinced us that GP had talented people, many good assets, and a culture with some very beneficial aspects.

To revitalize and transform the business, we applied the five dimensions of MBM, starting with a change in vision.

Vision

Prior to the acquisition, GP's vision was to be a low-cost converter of southern pine into valued products. Keeping costs low resulted in GP acting as a market follower rather than an innovator and leader.

Unfortunately, an ever-increasing rate of innovation by competitors—including new products, improved marketing through better analytics, new manufacturing technologies, and logistics strategies—was causing Consumer Products to fall farther behind in product quality as well as marketing and selling capability. This led to loss of market share and a deteriorating position with retailers.

To transform the business, we believed we needed to change its vision from "fast follower" to "innovative leader." This and only this would enable Consumer Products to provide its end customer, the consumer, with products preferable to those of GP's competitors.

Because the previous vision devoted no money to innovation, GP needed to begin investing sizeable sums to make up the deficit. In other words, it needed to build the capability to identify and understand unmet consumer needs, and then develop products and services that would satisfy them.

Another kind of innovation was to envision how carrying multiple GP products could create value for retailers. This required developing several important new capabilities, including the ability to demonstrate to retailers that buying GP's entire suite of products would increase traffic for them. This was one of the ways the other four dimensions of MBM would come in.

Virtue and Talents

GP in general, and its Consumer Products business in particular, had many talented and hardworking employees. But once the vision changed, it became apparent that different leaders and additional talent were needed for several roles.

It also became apparent that the many positive values we had observed in GP's culture should be broadened to include innovation, entrepreneurship, and knowledge sharing. Like GP as a whole, Consumer Products needed to embrace our challenge culture.

In keeping with the MBM concepts and practices you learned about in chapter 9, many existing GP employees were reassigned to different roles that fit their comparative advantages, enabling them to better execute the new vision. But given all the capabilities required to realize the new vision, many skills had to be brought in from the outside.

For one, GP needed a sales force that could sell to and collaborate with retailers who were not only consolidating but also centralizing decision making, and becoming much more sophisticated in their approach to managing their store categories (related collections of brands). Another need was for a joint business planning team that could connect our brand and private label products to the value that each creates for both consumers and retailers.

In addition, there was a need for a capability that further helped retailers understand and satisfy the values of their individual shoppers and that showed retailers how GP products would better attract them. Finally, Consumer Products needed an analytical capability so it could better understand markets and competition, and measure and improve pricing as well as all other aspects of marketing—including promotion, television advertising, print media, and digital marketing. In other words, it needed many more, and better, knowledge processes.

Knowledge Processes

When we acquired GP, Consumer Products had fallen behind in its products and technology, as well as in its understanding of its customers and markets. There was a lack of experimentation and knowledge sharing across the organization and an aversion to challenge at all levels. Decision making was hierarchical. There were numerous financial measures, but too few of them were actually indicators of long-term value creation.

After the acquisition, Consumer Products began investing heavily to generate superior knowledge in areas such as marketing and sales effectiveness. It also improved pricing strategies and operations. Rather than develop these capabilities separately in each category, GP developed them at the business level to improve knowledge sharing about best practices and experimentation that would benefit the entire business and be scalable with growth.

In the past, Consumer Products had been successful in growing with high-growth mass retailers and club-channel retailers. By sharing and applying knowledge from across GP and outside the company, Consumer Products began to grow with grocery retailers, with the untapped do-it-yourself retailers, and with emerging e-commerce channels.

Since our approach to knowledge sharing was new for GP, it took some time and effort to make it work. The introduction of the joint business planning process is a good example. It focused on bringing retailers the best knowledge on how to understand consumer behavior; achieve positive results from product selection, merchandising, and marketing investments; and improve returns for both the retailer and GP—no easy task. But once the kinks were ironed out, these knowledge systems helped Consumer Products change the conversation and improve the division's perception among its important retail customers, such as Costco, Walmart (and Sam's Club), Kroger, Dollar General, Publix, Target, and Family Dollar, to name a few.

As a result, GP's image was transformed from being the "worst" partner to being a valued collaborator with significant knowledge about how to improve a retailer's business.

Decision Rights

As we worked to apply the dimensions of MBM to the Consumer Products business, it became apparent that many GP employees were in roles that didn't fit their comparative advantages. Authority levels were not delegated to those who had the best knowledge, and often decisions were made according to what was budgeted rather than through a robust evaluation of the marginal value of the expenditure. Unbudgeted items received more scrutiny for approval despite often being less important.

RR&Es were not clear, leading to a tragedy of the commons. Too many decisions were being made in silos based on what was best for each part, rather than what was best for the entire company.

Until these problems were corrected, there was no way employees could spontaneously contribute in a way that was best for the whole. To correct this, Consumer Products began working to ensure its roles were filled by the right people. It clarified responsibilities and changed authorities so decisions could be made by those with the best knowledge.

This included setting decision rights for category leaders (those who oversee multiple brands) and brand managers, empowering them to make decisions that could maximize the business as a whole. Category leaders were assigned responsibility for improving market knowledge and sharing it with brand managers, operations, sales, marketing, distribution, R&D, and all support groups.

All of this may sound simple and sensible, but in reality it required a complete transformation in the mental models of senior leaders, who had been making most of the decisions. They learned that they could create greater value and get better decisions by acquiring the right talent, asking the right questions, fostering a challenge environment, and then empowering and rewarding their people.

Incentives

Prior to MBM, GP tended to reward people for meeting budgetary and quarterly projections, rather than for contributing to long-term value creation. People were paid according to pay grades, and bonuses were formula-based and capped.

Employees were penalized when they failed to make budget, and rewards were limited when they succeeded. Short-term incentives discouraged them from experimenting and innovating.

Now employees are rewarded according to their contribution to the long-term value of the business. This includes not only current earnings and return on capital, but their contribution to building capabilities for the long term. Leaders, in particular, are rewarded for improving the culture by applying the MBM Guiding Principles. Pay grades have been eliminated and bonuses—which are no longer capped—are determined by using both objective and subjective factors. Before, sales force incentives were based on volume. Now they are based on long-term profitability, improved relations with customers, and the value created for those customers.

Thanks to the employees who embraced MBM, applying this transformation process has made the Consumer Products business more productive and dynamic. The business has a much brighter future now that people throughout the organization are doing the right thing without being told.

This transformation is a valuable lesson for us all. Complacency and defense of the status quo are surefire prescriptions for business failure, because creative destruction is always with us. Even after transforming its approach, GP Consumer Products still has much more to do, because new competitors with good quality and lower costs are constantly entering the market.

Of course, value-creating innovation takes not only good ideas but timely execution, which requires all five dimensions of MBM working in concert.

Businesses with good ideas but poor execution ultimately fail. As ever, either we quickly innovate to meet or exceed our competitors' performance, or we'll be driven out of business. As shown in this case study, using the transformative power of the five dimensions of the MBM framework is one proven method for ensuring we are on the right side of that inexorable process.

GP's Quilted Northern Ultra Plush was named the top nonfood product launch of 2008, generating more than $135 million in its first year of sales. In 2009, Angel Soft Bathroom Tissue became the first GP brand to ring up $1 billion in net revenue in a fifty-two-week period. That same year, Consumer Products' net earnings (before subtracting interest, taxes, depreciation, and amortization) were 85 percent higher than they were in 2005—greatly exceeding the goals GP had set prior to the acquisition.

Georgia-Pacific's Consumer Products business is in a much better place today as a result of applying MBM. It is now more profitable, and its leaders and employees have a much better understanding of what needs to be done to create long-term value for customers, the company, and society.

Case Study #2: Insurance at Koch

Since the early 2000s, MBM's Problem-Solving Process has been applied to our insurance activities with great benefit—with savings of several hundred million dollars in premiums (net of uninsured losses).

Insurance is valuable to companies in that it provides a capital safety net for low probability but costly events. As such it is most beneficial to companies with concentrated risk profiles, limited capital, significant debt obligations, or other needs for reduced earnings volatility. However, insurance is seldom a profitable long-term investment.

In part, this is because insurance companies price insurance to cover their expected losses plus overhead, transaction costs, and profit margin. On average, we estimate that insurance premiums exceed the cost of losses by about 40 percent (a percentage that includes the fact that premiums are typically invested several years prior to a claim). So how did we at Koch apply MBM to make our approach to insurance consistent with our risk philosophy—turning something that could be viewed as a necessary evil into an excellent generator of good profit?

Vision

By changing our vision from buying standard levels of third-party insurance to only buying it when it benefits long term or is required by the law (or a customer or supplier), Koch has created a profitable insurance program that is very different from common industry practice.

For one, focusing on preventing losses through our risk management philosophy has also helped reinforce the need for operations excellence, leading to improved safety, environmental, and operating performance at our facilities. Thanks to improved operating performance, our incident rates have dropped significantly below those of the average company in the insurance pool, making a traditional approach to insurance even less appealing.

We have also applied the same vision to identify and evaluate forms of "embedded" insurance—the hidden economic risk mitigation that comes from modifying general business activities—which is pervasive in many companies. Embedded insurance includes carrying extra spare parts, additional inventory, or other redundancies to ensure against outages as well as compensating counterparties for sharing our risks.

Anytime we incur a cost or give up a return in order to reduce the likelihood and consequences of certain risks, we are making a decision that, from an economic perspective, is similar to buying insurance. In some cases, this embedded insurance may be profitable; in others, not. Our insurance vision encourages employees to do that analysis.

Virtue and Talents

Years of significant work were required to capture the value of our revised vision around insurance. Aligning a diverse set of employees around a common vision and risk philosophy was necessary but not easy.

Our revised vision is largely a bet on the operation's excellence and risk optimization capabilities of our leaders.

Because we are engaged in so many large capital projects, it is particularly important that we identify and evaluate the profitability of embedded insurance costs in contractor agreements. We have found that the most effective way to minimize these costs is to not select contractors on the basis of how much risk they will absorb.

Instead we focus on hiring the contractor most capable of doing a quality project on time and on budget. When we have selected contractors on the basis of who is willing to absorb the most risk in the contract, we have usually paid a "double cost" in doing so: once, in the price charged to compensate for the extra risk they are absorbing, and again in the losses we suffer from the delays and overruns that they can't afford to compensate us for.

So we are better off accepting the risk with a quality contractor than pretending we are protected by using a less able contractor who agrees to embed insurance in the contract.

Knowledge Processes

Truly understanding Koch's risks and knowing where outside insurance might be valuable helped optimize our insurance programs. Using marginal analysis, we were able to understand the economics associated with various insurance programs and identify the structures that created long-term value for Koch.

We found that the value of insurance is diminished by the fact that (a) uninsured losses are generally tax deductible; (b) only a limited amount of coverage is available; (c) insurance recoveries often occur years after the premium is paid; and (d) large insurance claims are often subject to negotiation and litigation. Because of these factors, the value realized from insurance can be as little as 50 percent of the face value of the policy.

Even though we have discontinued all third-party insurance programs, except those we believe are profitable given the actual risks, we still maintain external knowledge networks to continually reassess the merits of our insurance approach. This helps us identify and learn from industry incidents and trends so we can continually improve our risk profile.

Decision Rights

Because individual Koch business leaders have the best knowledge about the risks in their business and are best positioned to understand the cost/benefit trade-offs, they are responsible for appropriately optimizing risk.

However, decision rights for purchasing traditional insurance typically are held at the corporate level or by the boards of Koch companies. This guarantees that any insurance purchases are based on considerations of the risk profile of Koch as a whole. Insurance is for the benefit of Koch, not the individual operating business, so we align those decision rights accordingly.

With respect to embedded insurance, decision rights are dispersed throughout the businesses. This heightens the need for broad education and understanding; otherwise, we cannot identify and evaluate situations in a way that ensures consistently profitable decision making.

Incentives

Because individual employees and leaders usually have different risk tolerances than those of Koch Industries as a whole, we make a point of educating everyone about the company's risk philosophy. This discipline is important because, while individual decisions that are inconsistent with the company's risk philosophy may seem immaterial, in the aggregate they are not.

Any financial losses from an incident, such as a fire, are the responsibility of the particular Koch company—so the incentive compensation of its leaders is reduced accordingly. This aligns incentives, ensuring that each company understands its risks and is managing them appropriately. On the other hand, having each business bear the cost of an incident is more profitable over time, so employees also benefit long term from the higher profitability.

We have learned that purchasing insurance can provide a false sense of security that diminishes appropriate risk evaluation and mitigation. Removing that security blanket while holding leaders accountable for results creates the incentive to achieve good risk understanding and profitable mitigation.

Our insurance philosophy is beneficial not only to Koch, but to our customers, our employees, and our communities. By actively working to prevent an adverse event—like a fire or accident—rather than relying on a financial instrument that doesn't reduce the probability of occurrence, we improve everyone's well-being, and earn more good profit.

Case Study #3: Corpus Christi Complex

Flint Hills Resources' Corpus Christi refining and chemical complex provides an especially instructive case study of MBM—having been transformed not once, but three times since Koch acquired it in 1981. Today, its sales are ten times greater and its earnings

are twenty times higher than they were in the years immediately
following our acquisition. Corpus Christi has indeed undergone
a remarkable transformation—one that involved applying all five
dimensions to drive change in the face of three separate challenges.

It wasn't always a rosy scenario. For a time in the 1990s, we
considered selling Corpus Christi because it wasn't profitable after
refining margins fell to—or below—"break even" for marginal refineries.

Fortunately the facility's leaders embraced a new approach that
enabled the refinery to remain profitable even in the worst markets.
And now it is positioned to benefit from the rapidly developing
Eagle Ford oilfield close by, whose production is more profitable
for Corpus Christi to run.

Vision

Koch's vision to expand refining operations and to establish a platform for growth in petrochemicals drove our 1981 acquisition of
the Corpus Christi plant from the Sun Company. We believed we
had the capabilities to greatly improve and expand both the refining and chemical portions of the plant. For the next seventeen
years we were very successful in making this vision a reality, adding major facilities in 1982 and a second refinery in 1995.

But when refining margins collapsed in 1998, the Corpus
Christi complex began suffering losses. This prompted our team
to create a new vision that involved changing the way it was con-
figured—to increase the yield of higher-value products, improve
reliability, and reduce costs.

All this was accomplished. The complex became profitable
again, but it was still at a disadvantage compared to other Gulf
Coast refineries that had made the investments necessary to run
heavy, sour crude oils.

Then, in 2008, the rapid development of a large new oilfield in
South Texas (made possible by horizontal drilling and fracturing)
turned Corpus Christi's configuration from a disadvantage into an

advantage. That's because the new crude oil coming to market was light and sweet—more suitable for our plant than for our competitors'.

We quickly updated the vision for the complex. The first step in achieving this vision was to build the organization and infrastructure needed to buy and transport this preferred crude oil. The second step was to maximize the volume we were buying by building the capability to move any excess to refineries in other parts of the United States. The third step was to modify the refinery so it could run even more Eagle Ford crude, rather than less profitable foreign alternatives.

Virtue and Talents

When FHR acquired the Sun complex in 1981, we made sure we had leaders in place at the refinery who were committed to the direction we were heading. To that end, when we acquired the plant at Corpus Christi, we reinterviewed all of its employees, as if they were going to a new facility or business.

We also held regular meetings with the plant leadership to brainstorm how to improve and expand. When we began asking for ideas, we got little or no response. Finally, a former Sun employee explained that the previous owners had not only refused to fund any improvements; they never even responded to requests. As a result, the employees had come to believe that requesting funds for improvements was futile.

So, over the next few meetings, whenever someone recommended an attractive investment, I would approve it on the spot—to accelerate the needed cultural change. This served as a catalyst that began to energize the organization around improvement and growth.

In 1998, to make our reconfiguration efforts effective, we had to ensure that leaders at all levels understood and committed themselves to the new vision, and that they had the capability to make it happen. Significant changes in leadership resulted.

Later, as the Eagle Ford field's size became apparent, we immediately began to add the talent necessary to acquire that crude oil and construct and operate the facilities required to transport it. Downsizing due to the difficult 1990s had left us way too lean to capture this opportunity without doing this.

Knowledge Processes

In 1981, we learned while conducting due diligence that Sun hadn't built knowledge systems to track the profitability of the complex's units, feedstock, and products. For Corpus Christi to improve and grow, we had to correct this. Then we had to continually communicate this information to the leaders, engineers, and operators, so they could begin to make informed decisions and come up with ideas.

These knowledge systems proved critical in dealing with the 1998 market collapse, and in bringing about the necessary transformation of the complex. To guide us in this undertaking, we began to not only evaluate the profitability of each unit, feedstock, and product with current pricing, but also did so using worst-case pricing. These measures guided us in designing the restructuring so that the business would be profitable under all market conditions.

As you'll recall from chapter 8, creating good knowledge systems often requires building relationships with external partners for the purpose of gaining and sharing valuable information. When the Eagle Ford field was discovered, we didn't know how to assess the producers' bullish accounts of its abundance. In order to be prepared for realistic future production, we contracted with a knowledgeable third party to verify those projections.

The bullish accounts turned out to be accurate. We had hoped Eagle Ford might produce as much as 1 million barrels a day, but in fact it could produce double that. Knowing this helped us prepare for such volume before competitors did.

Another major issue at the time was the extreme lightness of

Eagle Ford crude. While Corpus Christi was designed for light crudes, Eagle Ford's was *too* light for the plant to run without blending it with heavier ones. If not handled properly, these blends can cause the formation of solids that adversely affect the refining process.

To help prevent this, employees from our Pine Bend refinery shared their knowledge and experience in dealing with similar problems involving other blends. After discovering that existing analytical methods for detecting the potential for solids formation were inadequate, our labs developed proprietary methods that would do so.

Decision Rights

Sun had structured Corpus Christi so that management made all the decisions without much input from the employees. Changing the decision rights structure to use the best knowledge from every source was one of our first steps. To make this possible, we strove to ensure the right person was in the right role throughout the organization.

When the refined products market collapsed in 1998, we repeated the entire exercise of evaluating the suitability of employees in their roles, as the business's needs significantly changed. We updated RREs throughout the plant to align them with the new vision. We also reduced authorities for capital expenditures, given the poor profitability in the industry.

A decade later, as Eagle Ford developed, our first priority became to identify a well-qualified leader whose sole responsibility would be to maximize our purchases of Eagle Ford crude and ensure the facilities were in place to transport it to Corpus. Given the importance of this effort, we selected the individual who was leading crude oil supply and product sales for all of FHR. We then set clear decision rights for him and everyone else involved in capturing this opportunity.

Incentives

The final piece in transforming the culture from what it had been under Sun involved establishing financial rewards for those who contributed to achieving our vision of substantially improving and expanding the complex, and using it as a platform for building a significant petrochemical business.

We quickly structured incentive and performance pay to reward those who helped realize the new vision. As a result, when the crisis hit in 1998, everyone was willing to do whatever was necessary to make the complex viable under adverse market conditions.

Today, employees throughout the organization understand the magnitude of the opportunity Eagle Ford presents and what it can do for the long-term future of their business, so everyone is working hard to fully capture the benefit of it.

Remember that the purpose of our incentive system at Koch is to motivate employees to be entrepreneurial, to create value for customers, society, and the company, and to understand that making the most good long-term profit for Koch will benefit them as individuals. When the incentive system helps accomplish these goals, MBM's whole framework produces results.

Thanks to the application of MBM (three times over), and the development of the Eagle Ford field, this facility is now much less reliant on foreign crude (down to less than 15 percent today from 65 percent just five years ago). This, along with all the other improvements, has greatly increased the profitability of the business.

Case Study #4:
Georgia-Pacific Green Bay Broadway Mill

"Oh boy, here comes another one."

That is how employees of the Green Bay Broadway Mill reacted when MBM was introduced in 2008. Since its founding in 1919 as the Fort Howard Mill, this Wisconsin facility had endured numerous ownership changes—each with its own management approach and culture—before becoming the GP Green Bay Broadway Mill in 2000.

Since our acquisition of GP, the Broadway Mill team had spent considerable time, as had all GP facilities, in working to reduce injuries in the workplace. While there had been steady improvement, the team wasn't happy with their rate of improvement or their absolute performance level.

After becoming part of Koch Industries, the leadership team devoted time to learning about MBM and how to apply it. Two years later, in the fall of 2008, an employee of the mill experienced a serious injury, highlighting that any progress to date was neither sufficient nor acceptable. Tragically, a college student working in the mill lost the end of one of his fingers. His mother worked at the mill too, and the entire workforce rallied around the family.

Following the injury, the team concluded that safety would be the best place to start applying MBM, specifically the Problem-Solving Process. They began by identifying hazards and then making it a priority to prevent injuries before they occurred. The results were remarkable. From 2007 to 2010, the number of annual recordable injuries declined from thirty-seven to nine.

Impressive as this was, there were further benefits from the skills they learned in this application of the Problem-Solving Process. Equipment failures dropped by 50 percent, and the amount of tissue produced per employee increased by 20 percent. This shouldn't be surprising, since keeping people safe correlates with the other aspects of creating value.

As employees saw the safety benefits of MBM's Guiding Principles and its five dimensions, they began to apply these concepts in other ways. They saw how applying MBM could be used to improve quality, reliability, cost, and productivity, too.

They took ownership for their work areas, assets, and personal performance while holding themselves and coworkers accountable.

The benefits of this quickly became apparent. To them, this was proof positive that MBM was truly different, not just another management mantra du jour.

Vision

It was a change in Green Bay's vision for safety that started all of this.

The Green Bay team decided to aim for an environment in which no one could ever be hurt. This was a radical change. Under the old vision, employees just accepted that they worked in a dangerous environment. They assumed accidents were bound to happen, so their goal was to be the best in the industry rather than accident-free. But following the accident, it became clear that "best in the industry" was simply not a sufficient standard for protecting their employees.

Early on, they realized that a key to making this change from "better than everyone else" to "accident-free" was not only to allow, but *to require* employees to stop trying to repair a machine while it was operating. Prior to the implementation of this vision, shutting down a machine was at times criticized, due to the costs involved in lost production. Now, production was no longer the most important thing—safety was. So employees could trust that stopping operations was the right thing to do.

The change in our safety vision led not only to improved safety, but to a change in the overall vision that helped improve everything.

Virtue and Talents

The mill's leaders recognized the challenge in getting everyone to internalize MBM, but the process turned out to be even more difficult and time-consuming than they anticipated. Some of what they tried didn't work, and mistakes were made.

One of the key lessons was the need to ensure that all employees acted in alignment with the Guiding Principles at all times. So senior leaders had regular meetings with front line supervisors to impress on them this responsibility. In turn, the supervisors took MBM to the factory floor in the form of daily applications. They recognized it was necessary to set an example and expectations for their employees.

Truth be told, this process was complicated by the fact that some managers didn't mind having a command-and-control system in place, one in which the manager always knows best and the employee was expected to do as he was told.

To change this, input was solicited from all employees. Direct reports finally got to let the boss know exactly what they thought. This was an important part of transforming the culture, albeit a difficult one.

As supervisors improved, employees made a commitment to each other that they were going to use and practice MBM every day and give each other feedback on how they were doing.

Knowledge Processes

As employees assumed more ownership for their operations, other tools were made available to drive improvement. These included internal benchmarking—to learn what had or hadn't worked in other GP plants throughout Koch. Then employees began to track their progress to ensure they were improving at least as fast as the others.

Another source of progress was creating a culture that encouraged challenge, as was implementing the challenge process. Previously, employees didn't dare challenge anyone who had authority over them. What the boss said was the law—whether it made sense or not.

Changing this kind of thinking was not easy. It required leaders at all levels not only to tolerate challenges, but to celebrate and invite them, and to prompt others to voice more and better challenges.

The walls and barriers began to break down as employees realized they could, in good faith, freely challenge decisions and practices—not only on safety, but on everything.

Decision Rights

Another breakthrough was when RR&Es were clarified for each person on the shop floor. Employees were then delegated the appropriate authority to make safety-related and other kinds of decisions.

Green Bay employees were encouraged to be entrepreneurial and to take action to improve the results in their work areas. Before, when a machine broke down, the operator would call a mechanic. Now, most of the time, the operators have the authority and are able to fix things themselves.

Passing decision rights to individual operators resulted in a culture change that went way beyond the operator repairing breakdowns more quickly. Operators began to take the initiative to improve all aspects of their business, including safety, reliability, quality, and cost—and thus profitability.

Incentives

Because performance improved, so did the financial rewards.

But the incentives established at Green Bay involved much more than that. With safety, avoiding being hurt or hurting others is usually incentive enough. Beyond safety, people became much more innovative and productive. They were doing something they wanted to do. They earned greater decision rights and were responsible for results. They were recognized and rewarded for their accomplishments. In combination, these changes provided powerful incentives.

Employees now realize they are respected and listened to, and that they are the ones who have made the improvements. No surprise, then, that their work has become much more fulfilling.

Many take pride in sharing their improvement stories with others. Many even say they are having fun.

The new passion inside the mill was evident when I made a point of visiting to understand their exceptional progress. Besides touring the mill and meeting many of the employees, I spent several hours meeting with the frontline supervisors.

At the end of the meeting, one of them referenced the mill changing hands several times in the past, each time ushering in a new flavor-of-the-month philosophy. He said MBM was different and consistent with his philosophy and he was willing to dedicate himself to it, but first he had to know if *I* was really committed to it.

"I ought to give you a hug," I answered smiling, "because I've dedicated most of my life to it."

The Green Bay story is typical of the transformation that is possible when an organization embraces and consistently applies MBM. It requires focus, discipline, and persistence to produce a culture dedicated to superior results. When a spontaneous order is created in which everyone wants to do the right thing and knows what that is, MBM works just as well on a shop floor as it does in a boardroom. And in doing so, it makes everyone's life better—a necessary condition for good profit.

CHAPTER 12

Conclusion

THE REAL BOTTOM LINE

Doing well by doing good.

—THE MOTTO OF BEN FRANKLIN'S
LEATHER APRON CLUB[1]

The bottom line of my business philosophy can best be summed up as follows: Good profit can only result from creating value for the customer. It is the manifestation of the entrepreneur's respect for what the customer values.

I am hopeful this book made that point at least half as well as Sterling Varner did one day in the 1970s when he blew his stack during a management meeting in Wichita. His eruption—or more precisely, the reason for his eruption—has become company folklore.

A group of us were meeting to review our crude oil gathering business. It turned out we were going to make more profit than usual from a particular deal, and a few employees at the table started joking and laughing about how they had outsmarted our customer.

Sterling, then president of Koch, was livid. "Stop it! You boys are way out of line! Our customers are our friends. They are the ones that keep us in business. And we don't make fun of or laugh at friends. It's not right. And if we continue doing it, we won't have any friends and we won't have any business. If we're going to have friends and business, we have to build trust by treating them with respect."

At that point, anything I said would have been anticlimactic. So I kept my mouth shut in silent admiration, cheering in my head, "Go on, Big Guy!" Sterling, as usual, had said exactly what needed to be said *when* it needed to be said.

Sterling was the right man to say it, because of all he did to create so many wonderful friendships for us. He might have started life in a Texas oilfield tent as a mule herder's stammering son, but he retired as president of Koch Industries and died a board member and stockholder. He was deeply grateful to his friends in business, and for the good profit Koch earned from them. And I was deeply grateful for Sterling.

There was no reason to have mixed feelings about this deal in and of itself—Koch had conducted itself honestly and openly, and our customer benefited from the transaction because we were able to provide the best service at the lowest price. So it wasn't the details of the deal that infuriated Sterling—it was the lack of respect and gratitude, the mistaken notion that the deal was the result of the brilliance of those who made it, rather than the capabilities we had built over the years to create value for our customers.

Those who believe wealth is accumulated only by exploitation have an extreme reaction to good profit, but in reality there is no reason to have mixed feelings about it. By definition, good profit is attained not through exploitation but through delivering value to others.

Good profit is earned through principled entrepreneurship—helping people improve their own lives. It is not diminishing someone's well-being, but adding to it by mutually beneficial voluntary transactions, based on respecting what the customer values. Such transactions are win-win, not zero-sum.

Some people focus on questions such as "What is Koch Industries' worth?" But this line of questioning fails to address the one thing that matters: Is Koch creating value for others in a principled manner? Our merit as a company—and the merit of *any* company, for that matter—should be determined by the answer to that question.

When employees have used the best knowledge to innovate and make good decisions, and when Koch has used MBM as a philosophy and set of tools to help us create superior value for our customers and society, the results and the good profit have been exceptional.

GETTING IN THE WAY OF MIRACLES

Throughout our decades of developing and applying Market-Based Management, we have rivaled Thomas Edison in the discovery of "things that won't work." Creating MBM has involved many more dead ends than throughways.

One such dead end has been the failure by some to recognize that MBM is a holistic system; that its real power is in its underlying philosophy and its integrated application, not in the form or the parts. Those who have gained only a conceptual or procedural understanding of MBM tend to not only misunderstand this point but to misapply it.

For this reason, before an organization can successfully apply MBM, its leaders must develop personal knowledge through a dedicated commitment to understanding and *holistically* applying MBM to achieve results. Gaining this personal knowledge starts with understanding the underlying concepts—and then changing your habits and thought processes accordingly.

This is a difficult undertaking. Given human nature, leaders and practitioners frequently fail to act consistently with their stated philosophies. This problem has existed throughout history for organizations of all types—governments, religions, nonprofits, and businesses. Such shortcomings result in cynicism, form over substance, bureaucracy, command-and-control, or destructive,

self-serving behavior. People attempting to apply MBM are not exempt from these failings.

Another mistake involves trying to apply MBM via prescribed,
detailed steps, rather than by teaching and reinforcing its general
principles and providing useful tools (models). Misapplications of
this kind put us in the same trap as the government's wasteful approach to regulation, mandating the exact methods to be used, instead of setting and enforcing science-based standards and leaving
it to individuals to discover increasingly better ways to meet them.

In conflict with our philosophy, some leaders have occasionally
treated relatively harmless deviations from an internal procedure
the same as a compliance violation. This is a fatal failing, since
MBM is effective only when leaders understand and apply it as a
set of principles rather than rigid rules. When they do, MBM can
serve as an antidote to the natural growth of bureaucracy in an
organization.

Due to the widespread influence and visibility of leaders, failures are almost inevitable whenever a company has the wrong person as the leader of a business, service group, or site. Some of our
biggest problems at Koch have been caused by keeping someone
in leadership who didn't exemplify our MBM Guiding Principles.

A different kind of problem is created when a business doesn't
develop a vision that is sufficiently specific or understood well
enough to be an accepted guide for the organization. To create a
proper vision, the leader must engage those inside *and* outside the
organization who have the diversity of knowledge needed to develop a constructive point of view, understand what the customer
values, and what capabilities are needed to create superior value.

This is why our project analysis process, the Decision Making Framework, is intended to be applied in a manner that is as
simple as possible but no simpler. Unfortunately, the DMF has occasionally been made so burdensome and complicated that it has
discouraged good projects. So, while knowledge gathering and
analysis is critically important, going beyond what is required to
make an accurate and sound decision is wasteful and can cause

missed opportunities. This can be easily remedied by the leader, who should ensure the elimination of all work that isn't important to the decision.

When MBM is applied bureaucratically as a rigid formula or a prescriptive process, it ceases to be MBM. To avoid this trap, we must keep in mind that the goal of MBM is to bring about a spontaneous order by establishing and enforcing only general rules so employees can innovate by challenging the particulars.

Other misapplications include turning MBM into a set of meaningless buzzwords—or worse, using it to justify what someone already does or wants to do. Another distortion is making concepts provided by management into ends in themselves rather than tools to help improve results, as in "charts for Charles."

To avoid these pitfalls, to truly make MBM work, we make every effort to select leaders who have the necessary understanding and insight to spot and correct these misapplications early on.

When people are first exposed to the overall foundation and philosophy of MBM, their tendency is to become overly focused on the words, the terminology and definitions. What works much better (after a broad introduction) is persuading them to take the time to understand a few concepts that are particularly relevant to their role, and then have them apply those concepts to real problems, followed by prompt feedback.

When new employees who are veterans of other companies are first exposed to MBM, they tend to quickly agree with the concepts and jump to the conclusion that their thinking and acting is already consistent with MBM. This tendency slows down their internalization and application of MBM. They make much faster progress when they focus on how different MBM is from their previous experience.

What works best is learning by doing. Yes, training is important, but only to get started. It cannot take the place of continual learning by trial, error, and feedback. We don't progress if we are afraid of making mistakes. Real-world experience is what creates deep, tacit knowledge regarding the effective application of MBM.

MISTAKES TO AVOID WHEN INTRODUCING MBM

When applying Market-Based Management in companies we have acquired, we have learned many lessons the hard way. Since other companies typically have a much different business philosophy and management approach, converting a company to MBM is a far bigger challenge than improving an existing Koch business.

When we first acquire a business, there are often so many gaps and opportunities for improvement (compounded by our need to learn the business and get to know the employees) that the tendency is to attempt to fix everything at once. This overwhelms those in leadership roles.

Here, as everywhere, we need to remember that it is just as important to know the order in which to do things as it is to know what to do. If you are attempting to apply MBM in your own organization—whether it's a team, facility, business unit, or entire company—I find a three-step rule very helpful: quantify, simplify, and prioritize.

First, frame and quantify (by order of magnitude of value) all the opportunities and problems you face. Then use this quantification to reduce the list to a manageable number. Finally, prioritize it according to urgency and magnitude.

After this is done, consider the following general approach when introducing MBM:

- Conduct an introductory MBM seminar for senior leaders.
- Disseminate copies of this book throughout the organization to answer questions, stimulate discussion, and prepare employees for engagement.
- When feasible, place a leader with experience in applying MBM in businesses, capabilities, and sites where you are ready to introduce MBM and include adoption of MBM in her RR&Es. This will greatly accelerate progress. Human

resources, compliance, legal, and business development can be particularly helpful in implementing MBM.

- Provide training and coaching for senior leaders to enable them to gain sufficient understanding to introduce MBM, including personally mentoring employees in the Guiding Principles.
- Perform an assessment of the culture to identify gaps and set priorities for closing them.
- Constantly reinforce the idea that value creation is the purpose of MBM. Don't forget that endless learning of concepts without application is not beneficial.
- Apply MBM to a few critically important challenges and opportunities. Early successes breed confidence in the relevance and power of the concepts.
- Get HR leaders to be active participants in the building and application of performance development practices.
- Ensure that the implementation of the MBM compensation philosophy is done in a way that provides inspiration and the desire to make a real difference.
- Introduce MBM mental models—such as vision development, comparative advantage, creative destruction, challenge, opportunity cost, subjective value, and RR&Es—selectively to those who can actually apply them in their work.
- However difficult it may be, remove leaders who do not have values consistent with the MBM Guiding Principles. Failure to rapidly deal with these individuals is not only dangerous, it creates confusion among employees and impedes progress in implementing MBM.
- Constantly make adjustments in pace and focus as MBM is introduced, and recognize the value of repetition.

I'll conclude this book by addressing some typical challenges from skeptics, such as, "Is MBM really a management system that can be exported?" And, "Is it really MBM that makes Koch successful, or is the company's performance CEO-dependent?"

And those are the polite questions.

In response to the second question, it should be obvious that I wasn't personally involved in solving all the problems described in chapter 11. In fact, on several, I only showed up afterward and applauded the successes. Many examples in this book, especially the chapter 11 case studies, demonstrate that MBM works independently of Charles Koch, of honest Midwesterners, inherited wealth, or any of the other misguided theories that fly around about Koch Industries' success.

One person cannot transform a large company's culture. It takes many people, and they must be persistent and willing to study and experiment. Widespread commitment to the integration of theory and practice is essential. (This is the essence of my alma mater's motto: *Mens et manus,* Latin for "Mind and hand.")

In response to the first question, I will merely say that while I might have been the one to piece MBM together—based on my studies, my life experiences, and some particular categories of intelligence—there is no doubt that fully committed leaders in *any* business can make it work. I have seen leaders in all sorts of roles in all sorts of companies do so hundreds of times, and I am delighted and honored when they do.

I receive a lot of mail (including death threats—153 of them in 2014 alone). What often makes my day are the many letters from former employees who tell me their opportunity to work at Koch changed their lives for the better. Many tell me this is where they learned what it takes to have not only fulfilling work, but also a life of meaning.

Among the most touching letters I received was one from Bud Snodgrass of Wichita, who worked for Koch from 1980 to 1998, mainly in sales and marketing for Koch Refining. Seventeen years later, he wrote to say: "Thank you for sharing your market and customer philosophy, which has gone far in shaping my own points of view not only in business but . . . my views of life in general."

He closed the letter by revealing something that places quite a responsibility on me: "You had such a very positive impact on me early in my career at Koch. So much so Sue and I named our first son after you. I know I never told that to you or anyone else at Koch."[2]

For someone like me, who was named for a person who gave my father a great opportunity, and who works hard so he can make a real contribution in order to have a life of meaning, this was profoundly moving.

And to those who continue to preoccupy themselves with the good profit that we have earned through Principled Entrepreneurship, I will say only one thing: I am certain that every business should profit solely by creating real value for others, and not at all by attempting to slow down "the perennial gale of creative destruction."

The main reason we strive to increase our capital and our business is to enable us to make a greater contribution to our customers, communities, employees, and society as a whole. That same focus will help any company create good profit as well.

The greatest gift we can receive or pass on is the opportunity to find and pursue our passion, and in doing so, to make a difference by helping others improve their lives. To be truly rich is to live a life of meaning. This was impressed on me at an early age and is a legacy I try to share. My hope is that everyone will have the opportunity to experience the glorious feeling of accomplishment.

Appendix A

KOCH'S MAJOR BUSINESS GROUPS

Flint Hills Resources
Petroleum refining, chemicals, polymers, lube stocks, asphalt, liquefied natural gas, grain processing, ethanol, and biofuels.

Koch Minerals
Bulk solid commodity trading and distribution, exploration and production, and oilfield and clean coal services.

Koch Supply & Trading
Commodity trading and risk management services.

Koch Pipeline
Crude oil, refined products, ethanol, natural gas liquids, and chemical pipelines.

Koch Ag and Energy Solutions
Nitrogen fertilizer, other plant nutrients, and enhanced efficiency products manufacture, distribution, and trading. Natural gas and power services.

Koch Chemical Technology Group
Mass transfer equipment, burners and flares, pollution control
equipment, heat exchangers, membrane separation systems, and
engineering/construction services.

INVISTA
Nylon fiber, polymer and intermediates, engineering polymers,
airbag fibers, spandex, specialty chemicals and materials, and
process technology licensing.

Georgia-Pacific
Consumer products, nonwovens, packaging, containerboard,
bleached board, fluff, market and dissolving pulp, structural
panels, wood products, gypsum products, chemicals, and
recycling.

Molex
Electronic, electrical, and fiber-optic interconnection systems.

Appendix B

BUSINESSES KOCH HAS EXITED

Activated carbon

Air quality consulting

Ammonia pipelines

Animal feed

Broadband trading

Business aircraft

Canadian pipelines

Carbon dioxide

Chromatography

Coal mining

Commercial lending

Cooling towers

Crude oil gathering

Cryogenic systems

Dredge manufacturing

Drilling rigs

European tissue

Feedlots

Fiberglass-reinforced products

Financial instruments, various

Gas liquids gathering

Gas pipelines

Gas processing

Grain milling

Grain trading

Image transmission

Meat processing

Medical equipment

Microelectronic chemicals

Particle board

Performance roads

Pizza dough

Platinum trading

Polyester, commodity

Propane retailing

Service stations

Slag cement

Sulfur plant design

Sulfuric acid
Tankers
Telecommunications
Tennis court surfaces
Trucking
Venture capital

Appendix C

PRODUCTS KOCH TRADES

Agriculture
Cattle
Cocoa
Corn
Cotton
Hogs
Soybeans
Sugar
Wheat

Energy
Electrical power
Emission credits
LNG
Natural gas

Fertilizer
Anhydrous ammonia
Enhanced efficiency products
Phosphate

Potash
UAN
Urea

Financial
Corporate bonds
Equities
Foreign exchange
Interest rates
Municipal bonds
Real estate

Forest Products
Plywood
Pulp and paper
Recycled fiber
Timber
Wastepaper
Woodchips

Intermediate Feedstocks
Ethanol
Gas oil
Naphtha

Metals
Aluminum
Aluminum alloy
Copper
Gold
Iron ore
Lead
Nickel
Silver
Steel
Tin
Zinc

Minerals
Cement
Coal
Exploration and production
  properties
Petroleum coke
Shipping
Slag
Sulfur

Natural Gas Liquids
Butane
Ethane
Natural gasoline
Propane

Oilfield Products
Chemicals
Guar
Proppants

Petrochemicals
Benzene
Cumene
Ethylene
Metaxylene
Methanol
Orthoxylene
Paraxylene
Propylene
Pseudocumene
Toluene
Waste fiber and polymer

Petroleum
Condensate
Crude oil

Refined Products
Diesel fuel
Fuel oil
Gasoline
Jet fuel
Resid

Notes

INTRODUCTION

1. F. A. Hayek, *Law, Legislation and Liberty* (Abingdon: Routledge, 1998), p. 136.
2. http://www.freetheworld.com/2014/EFW2014-POST.pdf.
3. Adam Smith, *The Theory of Moral Sentiments* (1759), 1.1.
4. Adam Smith, *An Inquiry into the Nature and Causes of the Wealth of Nations,* 5th ed. (London: Methuen & Co., 1904), 4.2.

Chapter 1: THE GLORIOUS FEELING OF ACCOMPLISHMENT

1. Letter from Fred Koch to his sons, January 22, 1936.
2. Letters from Charles de Ganahl to his son Carl, dated April 26, 1930, and published in *The Life and Letters of Charles Francis de Ganahl* (Richard R. Smith: New York, 1949), p. 380, and to Mr. Wilson Cross, dated March 17, 1933, contained in Vol. II, p. 667.
3. Letter from Fred Koch to Dr. Walter F. Rittman, January 30, 1948.
4. Ibid.
5. Letter from Fred Koch to Mr. C. A. Middleton, March 5, 1948.
6. Letter from Fred Koch to "My dear boys," January 22, 1936.
7. Cited in "Sam Walton: Bargain Basement Billionaire" October 8, 2008, from entrepreneur.com: http://www.entrepreneur.com/article/197560.

Chapter 2: KOCH AFTER FRED

1. F. A. Harper, *Why Wages Rise* (New York: The Foundation for Economic Education, 1957), p. 36.

Chapter 3: QUEENS, FACTORY GIRLS, AND SCHUMPETER

1. Joseph A. Schumpeter, *Capitalism, Socialism, and Democracy* (New York: Harper Perennial, 2008), p. 67.
2. Cited in "Joseph Schumpeter: In Praise of Entrepreneurs," Books and Arts section, *The Economist,* April 28, 2007, p. 94.
3. Schumpeter, *Capitalism, Socialism, and Democracy,* p. 84.
4. Ibid., p. 83.
5. Letter from Fred Koch to Dr. Walter F. Rittman.
6. http://www.freetheworld.com/2014/EFW2014-POST.pdf.
7. Based on data available through the year 2012. Authored by James Gwartney, Robert Lawson, and Joshua Hall and published by the Fraser Institute (www.freetheworld.com).
8. Thomas Hobbes, *Leviathan* (Boston: Adamant Media Corp., 2005), p. 84.
9. Adam Smith, *An Inquiry into the Nature and Causes of the Wealth of Nations* (Indianapolis: Liberty Fund Inc., 1981), vol. 1, 2.2.
10. Alexis de Tocqueville, *Democracy in America* (New York: Harper and Row Publishers, 1969), p. 526.
11. Richard Epstein, "The Limits of Liberty," *Reason,* March 2004, vol. 35, no. 10, pp. 40–50.
12. Vernon Smith, "Constructionist and Ecological Rationality in Economics," Nobel Prize Lecture, Stockholm, Sweden, December 8, 2002.
13. Franz Oppenheimer, *The State* (San Francisco: Fox and Wilkes, 1997), pp. 14–15.
14. Smith, *An Inquiry into the Nature and Causes of the Wealth of Nations,* p. 456.
15. F. A. Hayek, *The Fatal Conceit* (Chicago: University of Chicago Press, 1989), p. 77.
16. Thomas Sowell, *Knowledge and Decisions* (New York: Basic Books, 1980), p. 215.
17. Michael Polanyi, "The Republic of Science: Its Political and Economic Theory," *Minerva* 1 (1962): 54–74.
18. Ludwig von Mises, *Human Action* (Chicago: Henry Regnery Co., 1963), p. 32.
19. Thray Sithu U Ba Kin, "What Buddhism Is" (Rangoon: Vipassana Research Association, Office of the Accountant General, 1951), p. 4.
20. Schumpeter, *Capitalism, Socialism, and Democracy,* p. 84.

Chapter 4: OVERCOMING BUREAUCRACY AND STAGNATION

1. Cited by W. A. M. Alwis, "Spoon-Feeding in 'Do' Disciplines," *CDTL Brief* 3, no. 2 (May 2000), p. 5.
2. *The Deming Videotapes: Quality, Productivity and Competitive Position* (part of the MIT Video Series from the MIT Center for Advanced Engineering Study), copyright 1983 MIT.
3. http://www.forbes.com/quotes/author/mary-beard.

4. Ralph Waldo Emerson, *Essays: First and Second Series*, "Self-Reliance" (Digireads, 2007), p. 21.

5. W. E. Deming, *The Essential Deming: Leadership Principles from the Father of Quality*, ed. J. Orsini and D. D. Cahill (New York: McGraw-Hill, 2013), p. 105.

6. Michael Polanyi, *Personal Knowledge: Towards a Post-Critical Philosophy* (Chicago: University of Chicago Press, 1974), p. 159.

Chapter 5: LEARNING FROM ADVERSITY

1. Francis Bacon, "Of Adversity," *Essays, Civil and Moral,* The Harvard Classics (New York: P. F. Collier & Son, 1909–14), vol. 3, pt. 2.

2. http://www.fhr.com/ehs/performance_data.aspx (see Criteria Air Emissions).

3. http://www2.epa.gov/toxics-release-inventory-tri-program/2013-tri -national-analysis-waste-management-parent-company.

4. http://newsok.com/blm-finds-no-proof-koch-stole-indian-royalties/article /2311264.

Chapter 6: VISION

1. From the *Yale Book of Quotations* (2006), ed. Fred R. Shapiro, p. 315. First attributed to Goethe in William Hutchinson Murray's *The Scottish Himalayan Expedition* (1951).

2. Schumpeter, *Capitalism, Socialism, and Democracy,* p. 84.

3. Thomas Sowell, "Profits Without Honor," in *Ever Wonder Why? And Other Controversial Essays* (Stanford, Calif.: Hoover Institution Press, 2006), p. 82.

4. Smith, *Wealth of Nations*, vol. 4.8.49.

5. F. A. Hayek, *Individualism and Economic Order* (Chicago: University of Chicago Press, 1948), p. 101.

6. Ludwig von Mises, *Human Action: The Scholar's Edition,* Google 3-book (Auburn, Ala.: Ludwig von Mises Institute, 2008), p. 871.

7. Cited by Scott Thorpe, *How to Think Like Einstein: Simple Ways to Break the Rules and Discover Your Hidden Genius* (Naperville, Ill.: Sourcebooks, 2000), p. 149.

Chapter 7: VIRTUE AND TALENTS

1. http://sports.espn.go.com/ncb/news/story?id=5249709.

2. Frédéric Bastiat, *Selected Essays on Political Economy*, ed. George B. de Huszar, trans. Seymour Cain (Irvington-on-Hudson, NY: Foundation for Economic Education, 1964), p. 56.

3. Polanyi, "Republic of Science," p. 55.

4. John Adams's letter to the Officers of the First Brigade of the Third Division of the Militia of Massachusetts, October 11, 1798, http://founders.archives.gov/ documents/Adams/99-02-02-3102.

5. W. Somerset Maugham, *Of Human Bondage* (New York: Grosset & Dunlap, 1915), p. 254.

6. "Common sense is very rare," as translated by Theodore Besterman in Voltaire's *Dictionnaire Philosophique* (London: Penguin, 2004), p. 377.

7. Jack Clark letter to author, August 7, 2013.

8. Howard Gardner, *Changing Minds: The Art and Science of Changing Our Own and Other People's Minds* (Boston: Harvard Business School Publishing, 2006), pp. 27–42.

9. Jack Clark letter to author, February 17, 2015.

Chapter 8: KNOWLEDGE PROCESSES

1. Richard Whately, *Essays on Some of the Difficulties in the Writings of St. Paul, and in Other Parts of the New Testament* (London: B. Fellowes, 1830), p. 33.

2. Susan Hockfield e-mail to author, March 7, 2011.

3. Polyani, "Republic of Science."

4. Cited by Thorpe, *How to Think Like Einstein*, p. 3.

5. Michael Porter, *Competitive Strategy: Techniques for Analyzing Industries and Competitors* (New York: The Free Press, 1998), p. xiv.

6. Peter Drucker, "What Executives Should Remember," *Harvard Business Review* 84, no. 2 (February 2006).

7. Thorpe, *How to Think Like Einstein*, p. 35.

Chapter 9: DECISION RIGHTS

1. Aristotle's *Politics*, 1261b.

2. Garrett Hardin, "The Tragedy of the Commons," *Science* 162, no. 3859 (December 1968), pp. 1243–48.

3. http://blog.chron.com/newswatchenergy/2010/04/bp-ceo-on-gulf-rig -disaster-how-the-hell-could-this-happen. (The date of the CEO's remarks is April 28, 2010.)

4. Ludwig von Mises, *Human Action* (Chicago: Regnery Co., 1963), p. 311.

Chapter 10: INCENTIVES

1. Viktor Frankl, *The Unheard Cry for Meaning: Psychotherapy and Humanism* (New York: Simon and Schuster, 1978), p. 21.

2. Frank Dikötter, *The Tragedy of Liberation: A History of the Chinese Revolution 1945–1957* (New York: Bloomsbury, 2013), p. 270.

3. Abraham H. Maslow, *Eupsychian Management: A Journal* (Homewood, Ill.: R. D. Irwin, 1965), p. 28.

4. Abraham H. Maslow, *Maslow on Management* (New York: Wiley, 1998), p. 40.

5. Cited in Jonathan Hughes, *The Vital Few: The Entrepreneur and American Economic Progress* (New York: Oxford University Press, 1973), p. 149.

6. Cited in Zach Cutler's "Failure Is the Seed of Growth and Success," Entrepreneur.com.

Chapter 11: SPONTANEOUS ORDER IN ACTION

1. Frederich Hayek, *New Studies in Philosophy, Politics, Economics and the History of Ideas* (London: Routledge & Kegan Paul, 1978), pp. 63–64.
2. Daniel Patrick Moynihan, *Daniel Patrick Moynihan: A Portrait in Letters of an American Visionary*, ed. Steven R. Weisman (New York: PublicAffairs, 2010), p. 2.
3. Paul Arthur Schilpp, ed., *Albert Einstein: Philosopher-Scientist*, 3rd ed., Library of Living Philosophers, vol. 7 (Peru, Ill.: Open Court Publishing, 1970), pp. 659–60.

Chapter 12: CONCLUSION

1. http://www.washingtonpost.com/opinions/walter-isaacson-the-america -ben-franklin-saw/2012/11/21/8094bfca-3411-11e2-bfd5-e202b6d7b501_story .html.
2. Bud Snodgrass letter to author, January 8, 2015.

Acknowledgments

I want to recognize our employees who, throughout the past seventy-five years, have built Koch Industries into what it is today. In particular, I thank those who, during the last fifty years, helped develop Market-Based Management into the effective framework that has made Koch successful. I must also thank my brother David and the Marshall family, without whose contributions, loyalty, and support none of this would have happened.

Additionally, I appreciate the invaluable input from dozens of people inside and outside Koch that made this book possible. Especially important was the editing help of Bernadette Serton and Rod Learned, who did so much to make this book readable and digestible. Any errors or oversights, however, are solely mine.

Index

All of Koch Industries' proceeds from the sale of *Good Profit* are being donated to Youth Entrepreneurs Foundation. In keeping with Principled Entrepreneurship, Youth Entrepreneurs® teaches disadvantaged high school students the values and skills necessary for success. It also provides scholarships and venture capital grants, and arranges for mentoring by local business leaders. Founded in 1991 by Liz and Charles Koch, Youth Entrepreneurs' courses are currently taught in Kansas, Missouri, and Georgia. Plans call for expansion into several other states.